PASSION
—— FOR ——
JESUS

MIKE BICKLE

Charisma
HOUSE
A STRANG COMPANY

Most STRANG COMMUNICATIONS/CHARISMA HOUSE/SILOAM/FRONTLINE/
REALMS products are available at special quantity discounts for bulk purchase for sales
promotions, premiums, fund-raising, and educational needs. For details, write Strang
Communications/Charisma House/Siloam/FrontLine/Realms, 600 Rinehart Road,
Lake Mary, Florida 32746, or telephone (407) 333-0600.

PASSION FOR JESUS by Mike Bickle
Published by Charisma House
A Strang Company
600 Rinehart Road
Lake Mary, Florida 32746
www.charismahouse.com

Unless otherwise noted, all Scripture quotations are from the New American Standard
Bible. Copyright © 1960, 1962, 1963, 1968, 1971, 1972, 1973, 1975, 1977 by the
Lockman Foundation. Used by permission. (www.Lockman.org)

Scripture quotations marked KJV are from the King James Version of the Bible.

Scripture quotations marked NIV are from the Holy Bible, New International Version.
Copyright © 1973, 1978, 1984, International Bible Society. Used by permission.

Scripture quotations marked NKJV are from the New King James Version of the Bible.
Copyright © 1979, 1980, 1982 by Thomas Nelson, Inc., publishers. Used by permission.

Scripture quotations marked TLB are from The Living Bible. Copyright © 1971. Used by
permission of Tyndale House Publishers, Inc., Wheaton, IL 60189. All rights reserved.

Cover design by Bill Johnson
Interior design by Terry Clifton

Library of Congress Cataloging-in-Publication Data:
Bickle, Mike.
  Passion for Jesus / Mike Bickle.
    p. cm.
  Includes bibliographical references and index.
  ISBN 978-1-59979-060-2 (trade paper : alk. paper) 1. God
(Christianity)--Worship and love. 2. Devotion. 3. Jesus Christ. I.
Title.
  BV4817.B49 2007
  248.4--dc22
                              2006037759

07 08 09 10 11 — 987654321
Printed in the United States of America

ACKNOWLEDGMENTS

First, I want to express my deepest appreciation to Jane Joseph and Susan Van Leeuwen for their many hours of laborious toil at the computer. Blessed are these bond servants of Jesus who will surely be called great in the Lord's kingdom.

Also, much thanks to Judy Doyle and Walter Walker, whose invaluable writing skills and profound insights have significantly molded this book. What a delight to work with such gifted yet humble people.

Last but not least, to Stephen Strang, who first envisioned a book that would focus on inspiring in people's hearts a holy passion for Jesus. I'm thankful for the sweet times of fellowship with him around this subject that resulted in the direction to write this book.

CONTENTS

J esus said that the greatest commandment is to love God with all of our hearts, souls, and minds (Matt. 22:37). Actually doing this commandment is the key to all of life.

When the church loves God, it releases the power of God on Earth. The church will never "love one another" or the world until it first loves God. In light of this I am continually amazed at how little attention the church gives to this greatest of all commandments.

Christians demonstrate a consistent tendency to put almost any good thing ahead of loving God. Some of us make Bible study more important than loving God. Some of us pursue doctrinal purity more than we pursue the man Christ Jesus. Others put various forms of ministry like evangelism or caring for the poor ahead of the Lord Jesus. In some cases these good things even become a substitute for God.

Please do not misunderstand me. All of these things should be done. I do not believe that we can love the Bible or ministries too much. Rather we can love God too little in comparison with these things.

In my opinion, the greatest danger facing the church today does not come from without the church but from within. It is neither the New Age nor secular humanism that is crippling the effectiveness of the church today. It is the lack of love for God—the lukewarmness of the church—that is its greatest enemy today. A lukewarm, loveless version of Christianity may succeed in propagating a little religion here and there, but it will never capture the heart of a dying world.

What does it mean to love God with all of our hearts, souls, and minds? Some have tried to define loving God as obeying God.

Obedience is surely part of loving God, but we all know that you can obey someone without really loving that person. Love is not only obedience, but it is also passion. Obedience without passion for God is not love; it is only discipline. And if discipline is all we have, in the end discipline will fail us. But a man in love, a woman in love, will never give up (Song of Sol. 8:6–7).

Passion for Jesus will conquer a thousand sins in our lives. But how do we get passion, and how do we cultivate it? Why and how do serious Christians lose their passion for God? How do they find it again? All of these questions and many more are addressed in this book not only with skill, but also with a refreshing honesty.

Mike Bickle's book *Passion for Jesus* is filled with wonderful insights into the greatest of all commandments. These insights were not derived from an academic study of Scripture, but rather from the pursuit of a person. Mike has spent his adult life attempting, above all else, to acquire a consuming passion for the Son of God.

Anyone who knows Mike Bickle knows that insofar as he is consciously able, he has subordinated everything in his life to this one goal: acquiring and promulgating passion for the glorious Person who sits at the right hand of the Father in heaven. And therein lies the power of this book.

—Jack Deere, ThD
Author and Pastor
Fort Worth, Texas

AN AFFECTIONATE GOD

No one can come face-to-face with what God is like and ever be the same. Seeing the truth about His personality touches the depths of our emotions, which leads us to spiritual wholeness and maturity. Beholding the glory of who He is and what He has done renews our minds, strengthens us, and transforms us.

In John 8:32 Jesus tells us that we will know the truth, and the truth will set us free. We long to be free—emotionally and spiritually. Yet Jesus says that freedom comes with knowing the truth. And we must start where Jesus says to start.

Since knowing the truth sets us free, then what we know has a great impact on our emotional makeup. Thus, the way to our emotions is through our minds.

What truths must we know to be free?

First and most important, who is God? What is He like? What kind of personality does He have? Our ideas about God—who He is and what He is like—come naturally through our relationships with earthly authority figures. When these are distorted, so are our ideas about God.

I believe the greatest problem in the church is that we have an entirely inadequate and distorted idea of God's heart. We can experience short-term renewal through prayer and ministry. But to achieve long-term renewal and freedom, we must change our ideas about who God is.

In your most private thoughts, what do you believe God's personality is like? Your entire spiritual future is related to how you answer this question in the secret place of your heart, because inaccurate ideas of God will have a negative emotional impact on you.

For instance, if you are a sincere believer and you stumble in sexual sin, your heart is broken, and you cry out to God. But how does He feel about you right then?

The second truth we must know to enjoy freedom is who we are in God.

While both of these truths are vital to our living full and complete lives in the grace of God, we must begin by focusing on who God is.

BECOMING A STUDENT OF GOD'S EMOTIONS

David was a man after God's heart primarily because he sought to understand the emotions of God. His passion was to know about God and His heart. He wanted to know what wonders, pleasures, and fearsome things filled God's heart. He had many responsibilities as Israel's great warrior king, but he claimed that his first priority was to seek to encounter and understand God's beauty (Ps. 27:4). This reality fueled David's obedience. He had a remarkable hunger to understand the emotions of God, and as a result he had a unique grasp of the passions of God's heart. David was the Old Testament's ultimate student of the emotions of God. He was a student of God's affections; his primary purpose in life was an undying passion to know God's heart.

This single motivation empowered David. It must be the same with us. If we are to follow his example, we must have the same focus. By the grace of God, we too must become students of God's heart. We must understand more about how God feels. As we discover the same truths about God's heart, we will find ourselves living the way David lived and fulfilling the call of God on our generation as David did.

As we focus on His heart toward us and encounter His passionate affection for us, then we will become more equipped to overcome temptation. We will focus on four key elements of the gospel in our journey to understanding the fullness of God:

1. Who God is
2. What He has done
3. What we can receive
4. What we should do

The church places most of its emphasis on the last three: what God has done for us in Christ, the forgiveness and inheritance we receive as His adopted children, and what we should do in our walk with God. We need to continue teaching these truths faithfully. But the foundational element—who God is—is tragically absent in the church today.

The Holy Spirit is releasing much revelation in the body of Christ concerning the emotions of God's heart. He is taking what David saw in the heart of God and combining it with all that Jesus revealed about the Father's heart in the New Testament. People are listening to this message and developing steadfast resolve to become students of God's emotions, as was David, which explains the deep, worldwide hunger people have to experience God in nontraditional ways. But we will talk more about that later.

The great need of this hour is for the Spirit to raise up many preachers and teachers who are consumed with making known the personality of God! I'm not advocating imbalance, but it is the true knowledge of God that makes the rest of the message in Scripture so significant. A church that has not discovered the knowledge of the personality of God will inevitably be spiritually shallow and bored as well as lacking in passion.

This is not a book filled with formulas, such as "How to Achieve Passionate Christianity in Ten Easy Steps." Instead, it has to do with the powerful, concrete connection between *knowing* the truth about who God is as the way of *experiencing* passion for Him. It is the revelation of God's passionate affection for us that awakens our ever-deepening feelings of love and passion for Him. Simply put, we love Him because He first loved us (1 John 4:19). When the Holy Spirit wants to awaken love in us for Jesus, He reveals Jesus' love to us. As we see His love for us, we become lovers of God. Whatever we see in His heart for us is what is awakened in our heart back toward Him.

These precious insights into God's heart are near to every child of God. They are *within our reach!* They are there for the taking. God is accessible. He has made Himself available. The question is, how much intimacy do we want? Just how passionate for Jesus do we want to be? You and I are the ones who set those limits, not God.

The promise of being transformed and ignited to holy passion by understanding God's glorious personality is for everyone. No matter how weak or strong we feel, regardless of our previous failures, irrespective of our natural temperaments or personalities, each of us can be ablaze with passion for Jesus.

If the first twenty years of my life taught me anything, it was that passion for Jesus does not come from natural human zeal or enthusiasm. Passion for Jesus comes first and foremost by seeing His passion for us. Through frustration, condemnation, and heartache, I came to realize what ignites a heart with passion. The same can happen for you. It can happen to anyone who wants to experience passion for Jesus.

Let me tell you my story…how I started with human zeal and failed miserably. I want to show you how I gradually came to see God's affection and passion for me even in the midst of my many weaknesses. I believe you will be strengthened in your passion for Jesus as you walk with me through the following pages.

CHAPTER I

THE ROOTS OF HUMAN ZEAL

"Come on, Rocky! Come on … 492, 493, 494 …" I could hear my father's raspy voice giving me encouragement and could feel his thick hands grasping my ankles, keeping the calves of my legs pressed firmly against the floor.

"You can do it! 496, 497, 498 … All right, son! 500! You did it again! You will be an Olympic champion some day. All that hard work is starting to pay off. Here, son, let me help you up."

I felt his huge forearms, hard as iron, squeezing the breath out of me. I could feel his rough hands on my face, see his laughing eyes beaming into mine as he exclaimed, "Eight years old and doing five hundred sit-ups and several hundred push-ups every day! The guys at Waldo's Tavern are right; one day you will surely be a champion boxer like I was."

Ten years later as I read about my father's sudden death on the front page of the May 29, 1974, edition of the *Kansas City Times*, a tear splashed onto the newspaper article. Drying my eyes with the back of my hand, I continued reading. The article began by quoting two paragraphs from an article that appeared twenty-six years earlier in the *Times* on February 12, 1948:

One of the greatest comebacks in the history of the 13th Golden Gloves Tournament of Champions was made last night.

Bobby Bickle, a junior in Hoisington, Kansas, High School got off the floor in the second round to gain a well-earned verdict over Harold Stewart, amid the wildest excitement of the approximately 7,000 fans.

The reporter continued his article:

Bobby Bickle was the kind of man who refused to stay on the floor. In 1948 he fasted so relentlessly to make the featherweight class that he fainted twice at the weigh-in. Then he rose from the floor of the ring, dazed from a punch, and slugged his way to victory. He lost in the finals, but received the sportsmanship award of the 13th annual Tournament of Champions. As a lightweight, Bobby Bickle fought his way to the Kansas City Golden Gloves championship, the U.S. championship, and finally the international championship.

Bobby Bickle is dead. He died yesterday at the age of 45, apparently of a heart attack....

The words before me dissolved once more in a blur of tears. Gone...the dearest person to me in all the world was gone. Yet what a legacy he had left me.

The newspaper's headline that day said it all: "Bob Bickle, Champion of Courage." Yes, that was my dad all right. He was far from perfect as a man. He had many faults. As a young, tough, amateur boxer, Dad had been known for his unusual discipline and devotion to his sport. His goal was to be an Olympic gold medalist. Consumed with zeal and commitment to the sport he loved, he had worked out six to eight hours a day.

I couldn't recall whether it was in 1950 or 1951 that he had become the amateur world champion while in the military. During the 1952 Olympics in Helsinki, Finland, he participated in the boxing competition. The night before his fight with Aureliano Bolognesi of Italy, who went on to win the gold medal for the lightweight division, my father broke his right hand in a bar fight. Disgusted with himself for allowing such a thing to happen, but fiercely determined to reach his goal, my father fought the next day anyway. I heard his friends rave about that fight for years, listening in awe to their blow-by-blow descriptions of how my dad knocked the guy down three times in one round.

Failing to reach his lifelong dream of an Olympic gold medal hadn't defeated him or stolen his zeal. While in his twenties and fighting professionally, he was putting in eight hours a day on his job at the Chevrolet plant, and then working out six to eight hours every day on top of that. He was a man of unusual zeal and focus.

I laid the paper on the kitchen table and sat down, alone with my thoughts. I was flooded with emotion as I pictured my father in my mind: his infectious grin; the nose that had been broken and reset too many times ever to look straight again; the scarred, blotchy eyebrows, split open so often he didn't even need Novocain when they stitched them up because he had no nerves, no feeling there; that thick neck; those arms, solid as rocks, that had hugged me thousands of times.

My father had been very affectionate with me. This deeply marked my young life. He loved all seven of his children. He was always touching my face, loving on me, boxing and wrestling with me. He kissed all his children often. It was awesome. I loved it!

From my earliest memories way back when I was four years old, I recall him telling me how great I was going to be one day. He supported me 100 percent, and I sensed it. It was easy to bounce back when I failed because he was there for me. He was my main cheerleader in life.

By the time I was about five years old Dad was encouraging me to go to the Olympics. I was too young to know what participating in the Olympics meant at the time, but the idea of going excited my dad—so it excited me, too. He told me stories of his boxing friends

Jack Dempsey and Floyd Patterson, both heavyweight world champions. Dad called me "Rocky" after the great fighter Rocky Marciano. He had me working out when I was six years old. By the time I was eight, I was working out several hours a day. Athletics seemed to come naturally for me.

At ten years of age, my daily workout included running several miles and doing five hundred push-ups and five hundred sit-ups. Because of all the training, I held many athletic school records from my elementary days through high school.

I did not feel burdened to fulfill my dad's goals. It was not that I was striving to make him happy. I had confidence that he was already happy with me. I felt that I couldn't fail in his eyes. I enjoyed being with him so much that his goals just became my goals. I wanted to be just like him. Yet after training to be a boxer since I was six years old, at the age of fourteen I changed my mind and chose to play football. Instantly he said, "That's great, son. I want you to do what is in your heart."

My dad and I had a deep friendship, filled with affection and affirmation. I sensed the confidence that he had in me. He attended all my sporting events. If I was on the field, he was in the stands. While still only a sophomore in high school, I played on the sophomore football team, the junior varsity football team, and the varsity football team. I played three games a week, and Dad never missed a one. He even watched me during the afternoon practices. His commitment to my younger brother, Pat, and me was obvious to all who knew him. Pat was one year younger than I, and the three of us were inseparable. When I was about seven years old, my dad began working as a house painter. For years, on weekends and through the summers, Pat and I were by his side, scraping off old paint from the houses that he was to paint. At the end of the day we cleaned his paintbrushes and helped in other ways.

From the time we were little kids, Dad took Pat and me to the bars with him on weekends. He loved being with people. He was often laughing, joking, and causing a commotion in the bars. As a result of being in the boxing world, my dad hung around some rough people. Some were Mafia-types. Several of my dad's friends, whom I knew personally, were shot and killed in the underground crime world.

Dad's friends were my friends. Here I was, a ten-year-old, strolling into bars beside my dad, "high-fiving" these guys twenty to forty years older than I and calling them by their first names. "Hey, Jim!" "Hi, Bill!" "Way to go, Orville!" I was one of the "buds." They told me many of Dad's old boxing stories. I liked the barmaids, too, because they mothered me and gave me free Cokes. Pat, Dad, and I hung out together in the bars, playing shuffleboard, shooting pool, and playing the jukebox on Saturdays.

Although Pat and I enjoyed Waldo's Tavern, too, the place we visited most often was the VFW bar, a dingy, concrete block building that held maybe a hundred people. I loved the fish fry they had there every Friday night.

As we walked across the gravel parking lot, the air, always heavy with the smell of frying fish and cigarette smoke, was filled with music from the jukebox, loud laughter, and the sound of guys playing pool. The sound level always seemed to escalate when my dad walked through the door. His friends were the blue-collar, tattooed, truck-driver types.

Nobody bothered Dad. He was clearly the toughest guy there and the life of the party. People respected him for his eighteen years of boxing and all the championship titles he had won.

My family did not go to church. When I was fourteen, something began stirring deep inside me. I had often looked at the stars and felt an urge to figure out who was behind all the wonders in the sky above me. I would stare up at the sky and mumble, "There's got to be a God." One day I went to my father with an unusual request. "Dad," I said. "I want to join a religion."

"That's good," he replied. "I tried that myself once when I was younger." I could tell he was giving it some thought. "If I were you, I would either be a Jew or a Catholic."

I said, "Why?"

"Because the Jews are richer; however, the Catholics are bigger and more powerful in numbers and social influence worldwide. Either one would be a good choice."

I thought about it for a while. Then I came back and said, "I've made up my mind. I want to be a Jew. "

Dad smiled. "If I had it to do all over, I would make the same choice."

"Dad, if I'm going to be a Jew, how do I do it?"

"Look in the encyclopedia under 'Judaism,'" he advised me. "Take some notes, bring them back to me, and we'll talk it over."

I wrote up a short report and brought it back to him. He was enthusiastic. "That's good, Mike," he said. "Now go to the synagogue down the road from our house and introduce yourself and tell them that you want to be a Jew."

I walked into the synagogue as their Saturday service was going on. Then I realized that I was the only guy not wearing "a little hat" (or *yarmulke*). I walked up to the rabbi after the service and introduced myself.

"Hello," I said, extending my hand. "My name is Mike Bickle. I'm fourteen years old, and I want to be a Jew. How do I do it?"

I can't remember what he said, but he didn't seem excited about my decision, and he didn't communicate much warmth. So, a little dejected, I went back and told my dad, "I don't think they really want me to join them, so I will be a Catholic."

I went back to the encyclopedia, read about Catholicism, and wrote out another little report for my dad. On Sunday I walked through our lower-income, run-down neighborhood to the Catholic church. As soon as the service ended, I walked to the front of the sanctuary, past the communion railing, and through the side door that was just past the pulpit. I shook the priest's hand and said, "I'm Mike Bickle. I'm fourteen years old, and I want to be a Catholic."

Putting his arm around me, the priest said, "Son, that's a good decision! I'll help you!" The priest's enthusiasm encouraged me. He made me feel right at home at St. Augustine's parish. For nearly a year, Father Minges met with me almost every Saturday afternoon at the rectory for an hour or so to teach me about the Catholic faith. For every piece of information he gave me, I had ten questions about God, questions about the Bible, and questions about Catholicism. After some months, Father Minges decided I was ready to become a Catholic officially, so I was confirmed and baptized.

I was a sophomore when the head varsity football coach, Duane Unruh, invited me to his home for a Bible study. "You'll like it," he said. "Other guys on the football team are members of the Fellowship of Christian Athletes (FCA), and they will be there."

In June 1971, just before I turned sixteen, my coach paid my way to the Fellowship of Christian Athletes' summer camp at Estes Park, Colorado. He knew that my parents could not afford to send me to a weeklong sports camp. Roger Staubach, the famous Super Bowl quarterback for the Dallas Cowboys, was promoted as the main speaker. The night I boarded the bus transporting about fifty teens from Kansas City to the camp, my dad gave me a six-pack of beer. "Here, son," he said. "You'll need this." I shared it with the other guys on the all-night bus ride.

Roger Staubach spoke at the evening sessions and threw football passes to the teens in the afternoon. He deeply impacted my young heart. When Staubach talked about his relationship with Jesus, it was different from anything I had ever heard. "You can be born again and have a personal relationship with Jesus Christ," Staubach told us. That was the first time I had ever heard someone say this.

It was at that FCA camp, on June 9, 1971, that I went off by myself and prayed a simple prayer that changed the course of my life. When I told Jesus I wanted to be born again and to have a personal relationship with Him, I suddenly felt the warmth of God in my heart.

When I returned home to Kansas City, I had a newfound zeal to witness to my friends, but my dad was not excited about my new zeal for Jesus. This was the first time that I remember him being strongly against something that I was doing. My talking about Jesus bewildered him. I told him I would not go to the bars with him anymore. I told him that unless he and the guys in the bars were saved, they were going to hell. Although my dad's commitment to me didn't diminish, this injured my relationship with him.

I returned to high school my junior year wearing a nine- by six-inch wooden cross around my neck. I lugged a six-inch-thick Catholic family Bible to school. It was weird to my football teammates. They couldn't understand what had happened to me. Students were whispering, "Bickle became religious last summer and thinks that he is a preacher." My older sister Sherry, a senior in high school, cried as she exclaimed to Mom, "You've got to make him quit. He's humiliating the whole family, carrying that giant Bible and wearing that big cross." I did not have much wisdom or humility.

The next summer, I was invited by a Presbyterian church to live in their youth discipleship house with eight other guys.

The youth pastor introduced us to the Bill Gothard seminars, Campus Crusade, and the Navigators. I was hooked. I ended up attending Navigator and Campus Crusade meetings through college and reading their materials. I graduated from high school, and in September 1973 I was off to Washington University in St. Louis. I was in premed studies and on the football team. Things seemed to be going well. Then suddenly things changed.

Our college team returned from an away football game late

one Saturday night. There was a note on my dorm door to call my dad immediately.

"Hey, Dad!" I said, "What's up?"

"Mike, Pat's had an accident; he broke his neck and is totally paralyzed."

I caught the 2:00 a.m. train leaving for Kansas City and was there by morning. I could not believe that my seventeen-year-old brother's neck was broken. In a split second, he had been transformed from an athlete in perfect health into a quadriplegic who couldn't move a finger. He needed a respirator to breathe. I quit college so that I could take care of him. Within a month, Pat and I went to the Craig Rehabilitation Institute in Denver, Colorado.

The people of Kansas City surprised our family by planning a fund-raiser for Pat. A reporter for the *Kansas City Times* recalled the event:

> A double-header benefit game at Arrowhead Stadium, Nov. 17, raised $43,464. Bobby Bickle was there that night with his wife, Peggy. Bob Bickle stood in the glare of the stadium lights and looked out at the 20,000 persons who had attended the game. He thought of the Kansas City community that had rallied to the support of his son. The children who had sent pennies and nickels. The bankers and businessmen and football players and workers and farmers and people from every walk of life who had been there when they were needed. His eyes began to shine in the lights' glare. A powerful face moved to tears. "Man," he said roughly, "this is the greatest city in the world....Somebody needs to write a book about this city."

Pat and I stayed at the rehab center a little over four months so he could undergo physical therapy and I could be trained to give him total care. The nurses and therapists taught me how to feed and bathe Pat, how to make his bed, and how to turn him every two hours or so to help keep him from getting pneumonia or developing bedsores. They also showed me how to brush his teeth, how to exercise his muscles, and how to give him the medication he required. At first, Pat held up well. He is a fighter! But as the reality of it all began to hit him, I could see many unanswered questions and great emotional pain in my brother's eyes.

One evening as my dad spoke to me in a very personal way, his tone was strangely solemn. "I know you're only eighteen..." Dad hesitated, groping for words. "Mike," he said, putting his hand on my shoulder, "I know you love your God. Will you promise me before your God that if anything happens to me, you will take care of your brother for the rest of his life?" He was intensely serious. The thought of anything happening to my father never crossed my mind. He was forty-five years old and in the prime of life.

I clasped his rough hand in mine. "Yes, Dad," I said soberly. "I promise to take care of Pat all my days."

Some weeks later, my dad was going on a short trip. Just before he got in the car, I stopped him to say, "Dad, I love you!" He flashed that broad smile at me saying, "Son, I love you, and I'm really *proud* of you." Those were the last words my father ever spoke to me. That night he died suddenly of heart attack. The next day, the *Kansas City Times* did an article about him on the front page of the newspaper. As I finished reading the newspaper article about my father's death, I folded the paper and tucked it under my arm. It was a link to the dearest person in my life. Walking over to the window, I leaned my forehead against the cold glass, even though I couldn't see anything through my tears. "Good-bye, Dad," I wept. "I love you. I'll keep my promise to see that Pat is always taken care of."

CHAPTER 2

WHEN HUMAN ZEAL IS NOT ENOUGH

With my father gone, a new weight of responsibility seemed to drop on my shoulders. For a while, Mom just "spun out" emotionally. She felt such emptiness and loneliness with my dad suddenly gone. There she was, a young widow with only a high school education and a totally paralyzed son, five daughters, and me to provide for. My older sister Sherry was nineteen; I was eighteen; Pat was seventeen; the twins, Shelly and Kelly, were fifteen; Tracey was fourteen; and Lisa was eleven.

Fifteen years later, Mom told me that my dad had battled a terminal heart disease for three years before his fatal heart attack, but he hadn't wanted anyone to know. The doctors had already warned him before Pat's accident that his heart couldn't last much longer. I now understood why my father asked me to make a promise to care for Pat. How that conversation with me must have crushed my dad, knowing he was soon to die and that he would be leaving a paralyzed son and a large, young family.

Trying to cope with my dad's death and his own paralysis, Pat became severely depressed. I watched helplessly as the light in his eyes, once fueled by hope and determination, slowly flickered and went out. The day-to-day existence became more bitter than death itself for Pat. He began to hate life. By the one-year mark following his accident, my brother despised every moment of life—every breath. He was consumed with pain and frustration. He was totally paralyzed, totally helpless, and totally hopeless. He saw my face nearly twenty-four hours a day. That in itself was depressing to him. Every two hours—even through the night—I was turning him so that he would not get bedsores. So he took part of his frustration and anger out on me and on all the others around him.

The doctors warned me that such feelings of depression are common for people going through the various stages of grief. The paralysis alone was more than most people could have handled. Yet Pat was also grieving over the loss of his father while simultaneously confronting the fears and frustrations accompanying paralysis.

As I struggled at 2:00 a.m., half asleep, to turn Pat to keep him from getting bedsores, I was met with angry, stinging words: "You jerk! You idiot! Can't you do anything right?" I never knew when he was going to vent his inner turmoil at me.

I was not upset by Pat's words at first, but gradually I spoke back with angry and sarcastic remarks. I wanted to punch his lights out. Such anger rose in me that I would walk out of the room to cool off just so that I did not slap him. It would have really been bad if I had slapped my paralyzed brother! I felt guilty about the negative feelings I had toward Pat. I felt like a failure because of my lack of patience.

How could a real Christian feel as angry and selfish as I did? I had made a vow to my dad that I would take care of Pat. Yet within a year or so, things had degenerated to the place that I was continually complaining about taking care of him. I spent all of my days and nights at his bedside, but the tension between us was increasing.

Weary spiritually and emotionally exhausted, I had hit an emotional wall. Here was my younger brother, who had been blasted with twice the grief I was to endure. He was also working through the unresolved pain of my father's sudden death. I continued to try to mask the anger I had in my feeble attempts to serve my brother.

I had guilt over other areas of failure in my spiritual life. I missed my dad's affirming voice of love. I doubted God's love for me. After all, I had never failed my dad in the way that I felt I was now failing God. My heart felt as hard as a rock. I felt neither passion for God nor tenderness for people. I despised the commitments that my youth leaders taught me to embrace, such as daily Bible study and prayer. I hated prayer and Bible study, so I stopped doing both of them.

By this time, my mom saw what was happening and realized that Pat and I both needed some sort of change. So in September 1974, I enrolled at the University of Missouri, a two-hour drive from our house. I came home each weekend, from Friday at noon through Sunday night.

During my one year at the university, I sought to draw on the human zeal that my father imparted to me. I tried to apply it to my spiritual life, yet without much success. On the outside it all looked good, but inwardly it did not produce the spiritual results that I was looking for.

I wrote a daily schedule regimentation that included witnessing to at least one person, studying the Scriptures for two hours, and spending an hour in prayer. My youth leaders had given me Leonard Ravenhill's book *Why Revival Tarries*. One of Ravenhill's statements plagued me: "Any leader who refuses to pray two hours a day will not be worth a plug nickel in preaching." That sentence stabbed my heart like a knife. I believed Ravenhill was right, so I had decided to give prayer and studying the Bible another try. I committed myself to begin with an hour of prayer each evening and work up to two hours as soon as I could stand it.

I really wanted to please God and grow spiritually. Yet I seemed to be failing God at every turn. I was spiritually bored and confused as well as being filled with anger and guilt. I did not realize it then, but all the ingredients for an angry, self-righteous Pharisee were in place in my life.

For the first time in my life, zeal was not enough. If anything, it had turned on me and become my enemy—condemning me for my spiritual failures. I was being defeated by my inability to overcome anger, walk in genuine love, and develop real affection for God. Yes, I had risen to various challenges in my young life, but I could not change the spiritual dryness in my heart.

I was nineteen years old and a spiritual failure. What did God think of me? I could picture the anger, the disappointment, and the frustration that must be on His face when He thought of me.

I was failing at the vow I made to my father and to God to care for Pat. I did not understand how much sin I had in my heart—impatience, self-righteousness, unforgiveness, anger, self-pity, and lack of self-control. I did not have confidence before God when I prayed, only guilt and condemnation. My youth leaders assured me that God loved me, but *they* couldn't see the truth of how wretched my heart was. My spirit was beginning to become closed to God because of my guilt.

I was failing at prayer and Bible study. I continued to pray an hour a day—by the clock. But I *despised* it. What drudgery. How could I ever conclude that I loved God when I so disliked talking to Him? Frankly, many of the hours I spent on my knees seemed like a miserable waste of precious time. The Bible was boring and confusing.

I was becoming angry with God. My zeal to be a radical believer was still high, but my affection for Jesus had grown cold. I was still attending Navigator and Campus Crusade meetings and studying through the New Testament, but my efforts seemed dead. My head knowledge was growing, but spiritually my heart was shrinking daily. Instead of becoming more enlightened, I was becoming drier. Spiritual things had become so sterile—barren, wearisome, and tedious. I failed at fasting, too. I broke my regular commitment to fast many times in the middle of the "fast day." Yes, I hated fasting, too.

My human zeal was not able to deliver my heart. My increasing anger toward God and people added to my burden of guilt feelings. I was almost twenty years old by this time—and was a ball of frustration on the inside because I viewed myself as a spiritual failure.

I felt like quitting. My quest to love and please God seemed out of reach. I shuddered to think how I looked in the eyes of God. How could He like me? How could He receive me with affection when I was failing so terribly? That's when He spoke to me through His Word.

A STARTLING THOUGHT

One evening as I was reading the Scriptures, a passage from John 5 hit my heart like a bolt of lightning:

> You search the Scriptures, because you think that in them you have eternal life; and it is these that bear witness of Me; and *you are unwilling to come to Me,* that you may have life.
> —JOHN 5:39–40, EMPHASIS ADDED

I suddenly realized I was like the pious Pharisees who studied the Scriptures yet did not enjoy a relationship with the *Person* those very Scriptures were about. Like the Pharisees, I had been studying words on paper instead of cultivating an intimate relationship with a person. In fact, my heart grew colder and colder toward God the more I studied Scripture.

I was certain that my failure was angering God. I feared I was running out of time before He rejected me. Time after time, I found myself wishing my dad were still alive to provide the affection to which I had grown so accustomed. One day I stumbled across the story of the prodigal son in the Scripture. The verbs regarding the prodigal's father suddenly came alive:

> And he got up and came to his father. But while he was still a long way off, his father *saw* him, and *felt compassion* for him, and *ran* and *embraced* him, and *kissed* him.
>
> —LUKE 15:20, EMPHASIS ADDED

In the midst of my spiritual coldness and failure I had wondered how God felt about me. I even dreaded to imagine the expression on His face when He saw me coming back for forgiveness each time I let Him down. Suddenly I knew the answer to how God felt when I came to Him, for through the prodigal's father I glimpsed the face and heart of God. When God saw me trudging toward His throne with my head bowed in shame, I suddenly realized that He, like the prodigal's father, was moved with affection and tenderness for me. He was running toward me with joy. His arms were outstretched, reaching for me, longing to catch me up in His loving embrace.

My heavenly Father was a kind God who loved me. He enjoyed my friendship and wanted me to be with Him. A God who enjoyed me even in my failure and immaturity. A God I did not have to strive to make happy, because He was already happy with me. He was a Father who cheered me on and enthusiastically called me His son.

The awesome truth came streaking across my soul, bursting in to light up my heart with this truth! How could I have missed it? I had been struggling to please God so that He would like me, when all along my heavenly Father had loved me *as my dad loved me*—only far more! My heavenly Father had much more affection for me than my earthly father ever did. His love for us is much higher than anyone on earth could ever love us. David said that God's love is "as high as the heavens are above the earth" (Ps. 103:11, NIV). From that moment, I began my journey of understanding God's affection for me, which powerfully changed my life, replacing my guilt with holy boldness and affection for Him. I was beginning to enjoy just being in His presence.

SINCERE INTENTION VS. MATURE ATTAINMENT

During those years, in my zeal to please God, I had thought only of His holiness and how out of reach it was. When I saw my sin, I was confronted with my inability to change my heart. Like the apostle Paul, I had come face-to-face with my sinfulness and weakness. (See Romans 7.)

Paul was filled with passion for Jesus as a result of seeing the glory of His personality. For the surpassing value of knowing a glorious *Person*, Paul counted all things as rubbish that he might gain a deeper relationship with Jesus (Phil. 3:7–10).

I had zeal for God, yet without knowledge of His heart. (See Romans 10:2–3.) All that my human zeal had been able to produce was only a perfectionist performance paradigm and merciless self-condemnation. I struggled to reach the top of the ladder of spiritual attainment. But when I looked up, I realized that the top of the ladder, still far beyond my grasp, was leaning against an insurmountable wall of guilt, frustration, and powerlessness.

I lived under crushing condemnation as I struggled under the misconception that God had judged me as a failure. I felt God had rejected me. Yet God was not focused on my failures; He saw the value of my sincere, yet failed, desire to please Him. He was delighting in me. I was only beginning to understand His affection for me, even in the midst of my spiritual failure and immaturity.

The Father enjoys us each step in our journey of spiritual growth. He enjoys us not only *after* we grow up, but also *while* we are in our immature stage. My heavenly Father was enjoying me while I was yet in the *process* of maturing, not sighing in disgust as

I thought He was. He loved and longed for me; He enjoyed my fellowship with Him even while I was falling short.

Oh, the sense of anticipation that filled my heart as I realized that the Lord had real affirmation and affection for me. I began to feel confidence before Him. It was too good to be true! I wept for joy. And when the tears finally ceased, I could sense the bitterness, guilt, and condemnation beginning to diminish in my heart. As my confidence in Him grew, my heart became warm and tender toward God. Understanding God's great affection for me was beginning to reignite my love for Him. My little, flickering flame of human zeal was replaced by a blaze of passionate love for a glorious *Person*. His intense devotion and ardent affection for me far exceeded that of my earthly father's...and I knew I would never, ever be the same.

CHAPTER 3

IS YOUR GOD TOO SMALL?

Idol worship? I never would have believed anything could have made me bow down and worship before an idol. Well, it wasn't an idol exactly. Actually, it was a...no, I think I'd better start at the beginning.

It was the spring of 1972, and I had watched *The Ten Commandments* starring Charlton Heston almost ten times at the local drive-in movie theater. I was awed by Moses' encounter with God at the burning bush. After seeing the movie I read the Book of Exodus for the first time. I read it over and over that spring. I was fascinated with the story of Moses, especially the part when God said to Moses: "No man can see Me and live!" (Exod. 33:20). I quoted that verse often when they allowed people to share a testimony in the various high school Bible study groups. I warned those present that God was awesome and so powerful that to just look at Him would mean death.

During my "burning bush" phase, our Presbyterian youth group drove down to Dallas, Texas, to hear Billy Graham speak on discipleship at a weeklong event called "Expo '72" in the Cotton Bowl football stadium. He gave exhortations on the cost of discipleship, challenging us to evangelize the world. Fired by Graham's powerful messages, my friend Steve and I were convinced that God called us to go to Africa as missionaries that August—giving us only two months to prepare. We planned to quit high school so that we could go immediately. We knew our parents would be upset with this decision, but we were ready—or so we thought.

We were juniors in high school with no financial backing and no training. But the fact that we were both only sixteen years old was of little concern to us. We were convinced that God had called us, just as He had called Moses in *The Ten Commandments*. What we lacked in money and wisdom, we would make up for in youthful zeal. During the ten-hour drive back to Kansas City, Steve and I planned out the missionary strategies we would use to convert Africa.

It was past 10:00 p.m. when Steve and I arrived at the Discipleship House that we lived in that summer with seven other guys. They hadn't made it back from Dallas yet. We were tired and didn't wait up for them. Steve and I went down to our bedroom, which was in a pitch-black basement, and went to bed.

"Before we go to sleep, let's commit ourselves to God one more time to go to the mission fields of Africa," I urged piously. Closing our eyes, we each took a turn praying aloud. "O God," I prayed fervently, "we will surely go. We know how much Africa needs us. We know we are not yet trained, but neither was Moses. O God, please confirm this to us."

Steve and I opened our eyes, and then, suddenly, we saw a brilliant light across the room that appeared to be hovering just inches off the floor. It seemed to be as bright as the burning bush at the drive-in movie theater. Surely this was the confirmation we had prayed for. "It must be God!" We thought surely this was a sign, and we would be just like Moses.

Awestruck and trembling in fear, we crawled across the floor toward the light. "Don't look, Steve!" I whispered, sounding the same warning I'd repeated many times before: "Don't ever look at God, or you'll surely die!" In whispered tones Steve assured me he understood the principle.

We then knelt side by side and covered our eyes with our hands. Through the cracks between our fingers we could still see the glow of the flickering, mysterious fire.

"O God," I whispered, "send us to Africa."

Hardly daring to breathe, we awaited God's response. Several minutes passed, but we were met with nothing but silence. "Please don't look," I again whispered in Steve's direction, "or you will surely die!"

Once more, Steve assured me he understood. The seconds dragged by. "What shall we do now, Mike?" he asked softly.

"Pray a little louder this time, just in case."

Steve prayed, and we waited. When there was no response, we each took a turn or two at quoting different verses from the Bible. Again, we were met with silence.

I even tried imitating the British accent of one of my favorite preachers, Stephen Olford, as I prayed and quoted Isaiah 6:8, "Here am I. Send me!" But nothing seemed to be working. Finally, Steve could stand the suspense no longer.

He peeked.

Instantly, Steve screamed and fell over, landing on top of me, sending me sprawling. Hadn't I warned him not to look? Now the Lord had killed him for sure.

As I fell in a heap, I opened one eye and then the other. To my horror, I saw an ordinary, old water heater whose pilot flame had kicked on at the precise moment we'd asked the Lord for a sign. I didn't even know the water heater was in the closet because it had been hidden behind some clothes. One of our roommates had moved out the week we were in Dallas. Behind all his clothes stood the water heater, unseen by us in the previous weeks before the Dallas trip.

Embarrassed beyond words, Steve and I collapsed on the floor, promising each other we would never tell the story. You would be hard-pressed to convince either of us that God doesn't have a sense of humor.

Neither Steve nor I went to Africa that summer. After the episode of bowing down to the water heater, we opted to stay in Kansas City and finish our senior year in high school instead of going to Africa.

As young Christians we misunderstood many things. We were not supposed to go to Africa as missionaries. Our burning bush experience was only a water heater. But there was one thing we did get right: the glory of God is beyond anything we've ever imagined. Since my teenage years I have been gripped with a yearning to see Him and to grow in the knowledge of God's holiness and majesty.

In my late teens my mentors urged me to read books such as *The Knowledge of the Holy* by A. W. Tozer, *Gleanings in the Godhead* by Arthur W. Pink, and *Knowing God* by J. I. Packer. I devoured these books from cover to cover. My heart was warmed by the holy fire that blazed in the souls of these men who had unusual insight into some of God's splendor and majesty.

It is the knowledge of God as the holy One that fires our hearts with awe. I kept reading my Bible and those three books over and over. As I read, meditated, and prayed, the Holy Spirit took the hammer of truth and began breaking up some of the small and inadequate concepts of God that had been built into my life. He began to lay a new foundation, and the process is still going on to this day. My inner man is continually in the process of being renewed into a fuller, more complete knowledge of God and His glorious personality.

The church as a whole possesses so little knowledge of what God is truly like. I admit that this also is my greatest spiritual deficiency. Our ignorance of His majesty and glorious personality rots our religion. It leads to errors in our doctrines and contributes to the decay of our confidence and passion in worship. Our inadequate ideas about the personhood of God result in failure to develop deep affection for Jesus and to obey Him with fearless abandonment.

J. I. Packer correctly diagnosed this great disease in the church when he wrote:

> Christian minds have been conformed to the modern spirit: the spirit…that spawns great thoughts of man and leaves room for only small thoughts of God.[1]

Our faulty religious ideas of God damage our relationships with Him, deplete our prayer lives, and drain the joy from our sacrificial service.

HOW BIG IS YOUR GOD?

Our world is affected tragically every day by people who possess little or no sense of God's transcendence. Much of creation does not know—or care—that its Creator is unequaled, unrivaled, and supreme. Transcendence when in reference to God means that He exists not only in but also beyond our realm of reality. In other words, He's not like us—far from it. God is exalted far above His created universe, so far that even the brightest human minds cannot begin to fathom it. As Tozer explains:

> The caterpillar and the archangel, though far removed from each other in the scale of created things, are nevertheless one in that they are alike created. They both belong in the category of that-which-is-not-God and are separated from God by infinitude itself.[2]

In Old Testament times, whenever God appeared to men, an overwhelming sense of terror and dread was the result. When God spoke to Abram, His beloved friend fell on his face (Gen. 17:3). When the angel of the Lord appeared to Moses in a flame of fire out of the midst of a bush, Moses hid his face, for he was afraid to look at God (Exod. 3:2–6).

In contrast, many in our day are so blind to God's transcendence that they show shocking disregard for Him. If people are unaware of God's terrifying supremacy that transcends the universe and time itself, they will have little fear of Him. If we have no fear of God, nor the fear of consequences, then we will easily break His commands. The downward spiral of morality in our society is directly proportional to the loss of our understanding of the greatness of God. In the minds of many who believe there is a God, He is only a little more than an elected official—not to be taken too seriously when we disagree with Him.

Why does our society have such an irreverent and lowly view of God? The answer is simple. The church has not proclaimed it! The church's concept of God is much too small.

For many Christians Jesus is more like Santa Claus or a pop psychologist than the holy Other who will judge heaven and earth by His Word. The glory of God's personhood has not been clearly proclaimed to our generation. But when even the faintest light of God's surpassing greatness dawns upon our minds, we will walk carefully before Him as we work out our salvation with fear and trembling (Phil. 2:12–13).

Daniel, a man greatly beloved by God, was granted an overpowering vision of an angel:

His body also was like beryl, his face had the appearance of lightning, his eyes were like flaming torches, his arms and feet like the gleam of polished bronze, and the sound of his words like the sound of a tumult. Now I, Daniel, alone saw the vision, while the men who were with me did not see the vision; nevertheless, a great dread fell on them, and they ran away to hide themselves. So I was left alone and saw this great vision; yet no strength was left in me, for my natural color turned to a deathly pallor, and I retained no strength.... Then behold, a hand touched me and set me trembling on my hands and knees.

—Daniel 10:6–8, 10

Daniel was left speechless and breathless, and all his strength was drained from him (Dan. 10:15, 17). In the vision he was told that the Lord had sent the archangel Michael to fight with the demonic prince of Persia. The messenger in the vision Daniel saw was only another lower-ranked angel. What would it have been like to have beheld Michael or even the Lord Himself? Without doubt, such revelation would change our thinking about a lot of things. Our worship would be ignited with passion.

When we begin to comprehend the excellencies of God's person, we will be horrified by the declining ethics and decaying morality in our churches and our nation. Whether by insight and spiritual revelation or by visions in Technicolor, the effect is the same: beholding the holiness and glory of God reveals the presence of sin and its terrible ugliness.

Isaiah was probably the most righteous man in all Israel in his day. He was the prophet of God. Notice his response after seeing a vision of the Lord sitting on His throne:

> Then I said, "Woe is me, for I am ruined! Because I am a man of unclean lips, and I live among a people of unclean lips; for my eyes have seen the King, the Lord of hosts."
>
> —Isaiah 6:5

A new revelation of God's holiness always shines the spotlight on our own condition.

NO CONTRADICTIONS WITH GOD

Small thoughts about the personhood of God hinder our relationship with Him. Our ignorance of God's personality has also led to errors in the theology and doctrine of the church. The average believer is intimidated at times by words like *theology* and *doctrine* because they sound so intellectual and controversial.

Theology is simply the study of God and His relationship with man and the universe; doctrine is what is taught as the belief of a church. You cannot cast off theology and doctrine in order to be "simply Christian."

Incorrect views of God can create confusion and misunderstanding. For example, our imperfect knowledge of God has sometimes led us to imagine Him in conflict with Himself—His long-suffering warring against His wrath, or His justice wrestling against His tender mercy. As Tozer says, "Between His attributes no contradiction can exist. He need not suspend one to exercise another, for in Him all His attributes are one."[3]

If only more believers understood that God is immutable—He never changes. What He has always been, He will ever be. God never suspends one attribute to exercise another. For example, He never diminishes in His holiness when He exercises His love and tender mercy. None of God's qualities ever diminish in even the slightest degree.

In fact, when one immutable aspect of the nature of God is seemingly in conflict with another of His immutable attributes, it is at that place where you will see glimpses of His greatness.

Suppose there was a gardener who had planted and cared for a prize-winning bed of flowers. He would spare no expense. Which would the gardener hate more: a weed in the common field or a weed in the bed of his prize-winning flowers? Obviously, he would hate the weed in his flower bed more because it chokes the life out of his prize-winning flowers and destroys the glory of his handiwork.

In the same way God hates all sin. Nothing describes His abhorrence for sin in the wicked better than the degree of eternal punishment He prescribes for it. Nevertheless, He hates sin infinitely more in the lives of Christians because we are His vineyard, "the planting of the LORD" (Isa. 61:3). The most wonderful thing of all is that He loves us with an everlasting love and reckons us as perfectly righteous because of our faith in Christ and His work on the cross (2 Cor. 5:17–21).

I hate the sin of lying. But I would hate it so much more if it were found in one of my own sons. Why? Because I am their father. I love them, and they are called by my name.

When we begin to comprehend God's perfect and immutable holiness, and at the same time realize His unfathomable love for us, then we begin to understand His hatred of sin in our lives. The illumination of our hearts with the knowledge of God transforms us into that same image. A casual attitude about sin comes from an incomplete understanding of God.

The cross of Calvary was the greatest display of the character and attributes of God. God in His perfect holiness does not wink at the slightest sin. He did not say to Adam, "That's one! Don't let it happen again." It was for that one act of disobedience that Adam and his entire race fell.

I have often been asked, "If God is a God of love, how could He send anyone to hell?" But the more appropriate question is this: If God is a God of perfect holiness, how could He send anyone to heaven?

How can a holy and just God arbitrarily overlook sin? How could a loving God not forgive sin? Immutable holiness and unconditional love collide. But God would never violate His holiness, nor would He turn away from His love. The greatness of God was displayed, not in the fact that He forgave our sins, but in precisely *the way* He forgave them—He sent His Son as a perfect sacrifice for us. His love was displayed, and His justice was satisfied. The apostle Paul said in his letter to the Romans that in the cross God became both "just and the justifier of the one who has faith in Jesus" (Rom. 3:26).

Some have such a dim view or low appreciation for both the holiness and love of God that the cross does not seem that significant. They understand neither the greatness of their need nor the glory of God's gift.

Jesus taught that the one who has been forgiven much will love much (Luke 7:47). You will "love much" when you begin to comprehend the magnitude of what Christ has done on your behalf. Passion is birthed in you by revelation of the knowledge of God.

OUR PRAYER LIVES

An imperfect understanding of God's immutability has decreased the quality of prayer for many Christians and has led to misunderstandings regarding the nature of prayer. We cannot "twist God's arm" or throw a temper tantrum to make Him give us what we want. A wise earthly father does not respond to such tactics, and neither does our heavenly Father.

A more accurate understanding of the goodness of God can also be a tremendous aid to prayer. It is God's goodness, not ours, that is the basis for blessing. Understanding this frees us to place our confidence and trust in God Himself instead of being forced to rely upon our own righteousness or upon whatever faith we can muster. As Tozer said:

> There can be no merit in human conduct, not even in the purest and the best. Always God's goodness is the ground of our expectation. Repentance, although necessary, is not meritorious but a condition for receiving the gracious gift of pardon which God gives of His goodness. Prayer is not in itself meritorious. It lays God under no obligation nor puts Him in debt to any. He hears prayer because He is good, and for no other reason. Nor is faith

meritorious; it is simply confidence in the goodness of God, and the lack of it is a reflection upon God's holy character.

The whole outlook of mankind might be changed if we could all believe that we dwell under a friendly sky and that the God of heaven, although exalted in power and majesty, is eager to be friends with us.

…The greatness of God rouses fear within us, but His goodness encourages us not to be afraid of Him. To fear and not be afraid—that is the paradox of faith.[4]

I once saw a Dennis the Menace cartoon that illustrates these points. Dennis and his friend were walking out of Mrs. Wilson's house with cookies in both hands. Dennis's friend wondered what they had done to deserve the cookies. Dennis explained, "Mrs. Wilson doesn't give us cookies because we are nice. We get cookies because Mrs. Wilson is nice."

JUST A GLIMPSE OF HIM

I know people who are fanatical about our city's National Football League team, the Kansas City Chiefs. They know detailed information on every player, they keep up with every trade rumor, and they can recite the scheduled games backward. They meditate on it day and night. They press on to learn all they can about their beloved team.

So it is with those who are passionate to know God more. Those who want to know Him more press on to gain a deeper understanding of His nature and meditate on Him day and night. Those who do not press in to understand the depth of God's affection for us will eventually become spiritually bored and passive in their faith (Eph. 3:18). Their shallow understanding fails to capture their imaginations, much less inflame their passions.

The great need of the church is to see, know, and discover the indescribable glory of who God is and how He feels toward us. Seeing the heart, mind, and character of God will cure our compromise and instability and motivate us to bright righteousness and holy passion. Personal, experiential knowledge of the Person of Jesus will fuel obedience and zeal. It will put a stop to our restlessness and discontent. A new depth of intimacy with Him will extinguish our boredom and capture our hearts. Just a glimpse of Him...

John, whom Jesus nicknamed the "Son of Thunder" (Mark 3:17) because of his fiery temperament, became one of the most prominent of the apostles. As he walked with Jesus, John's fiery selfish ambition was replaced by fiery passion for Jesus.

John's own Gospel makes it clear that he was greatly beloved by the Lord. He was one of the three apostles who were closest to Jesus. He was allowed to witness the raising of Jairus's daughter (Matt. 9:18–25) and to be present at the transfiguration (Luke 9:28–36). It was John who reclined on Jesus' breast at the Passover feast (John 13:23). John was present at Christ's trial and was the only apostle who stood near the cross upon which Jesus was nailed. Just before the Lord died, it was to John, not to His own half-brothers and sisters, that Jesus entrusted the care of His mother, Mary (John 19:26–27). It is this beloved friend of Jesus who writes in Revelation:

> I saw...one like a son of man....And His head and His hair were white like white wool, like snow; and His eyes were like a flame of fire; and His feet were like burnished bronze, when it has been caused to glow in a furnace, and His voice was like the sound of many waters....His face was like the sun shining in its strength. And when I saw Him, I fell at His feet as a dead man.
>
> —REVELATION 1:12–17

Think of it. *The Living Bible* states that John was Christ's "closest friend" (John 13:23). But when the Lord, whom John had served faithfully, appeared to him in His awesome majesty and glory, John "fell at His feet as a dead man" (Rev. 1:17). Imagine a man of John's spiritual stature and experience being totally overcome by this brief glimpse of the beloved Friend he had served faithfully for more than sixty years.

When we are exposed to even a portion of His consuming glory, as John was, we will be motivated to live free from sin, die to selfishness, and give ourselves passionately to the Lord. When we gaze upon His loveliness, we will gladly die to those things that are not like Him.

John knew much about Jesus in His humanity and humility. He looked like us as He walked the earth during His ministry. Paul wrote that Jesus, who existed in the form of God, emptied Himself to the point that He was made in the likeness of men. He went on to say that now He is exalted to the extent that at the sight of Him, every knee would bow and confess that He is Lord (Phil. 2:5–11).

Although no one knew Jesus more intimately than John while He was on earth, the revelation of His resurrected glory caused John to fall at His feet as a dead man.

While Jesus walked on earth, His glory was veiled in human flesh. Veils were used in the Bible to hide the glory of God. A veil was put over Moses' face to hide the glory, a veil hid the holy of holies and glory of God in the tabernacle, and the writer of Hebrews spoke of the "veil, that is, His flesh" (Heb. 10:20).

In his letter to the Corinthians, Paul discusses one other veil that hides the glory of God. It is the veil that covers the heart and prevents a person from beholding the glory of Christ (2 Cor. 3:7–18).

The revelation of the true knowledge of the glorified Christ will transform you. Paul ends his discussion of the veil over the heart with this statement:

> But we all, with unveiled face beholding as in a mirror the glory of the Lord, are being transformed into the same image from glory to glory.
>
> —2 Corinthians 3:18

The splendor and glory of Jesus Christ, however, will once again capture the affections of the church in a new way. John wrote his account many years after the other three Gospel writers. As he looked back, he commented on the irresistible nature of the knowledge of Jesus Christ.

> His life is the light that shines through the darkness—and the darkness can never extinguish it.
>
> —John 1:5, TLB

The blazing light and majestic loveliness of the knowledge of God are about to shine into the community of the redeemed, and all the dark forces of hell will not be able to overpower it. Compromise and passivity will be solved as the Lord allows us to gaze upon Him with deeper insight into His personal beauty and unveil His glory. The body of Christ will rediscover Christ's personhood and majesty. When we do, we will give ourselves to Him in unparalleled affection and obedience. We will long to draw closer to God, hoping to catch just a small glimpse of His beauty.

CHAPTER 4

BECOMING FASCINATED WITH GOD'S BEAUTY

Ever since my brother's accident, we have been in and out of hospitals. In the early days of his recovery we spent months at a time in rehabilitation hospitals. Occasionally we would see a nurse fall in love with a patient. It did not happen that often, but every now and then, a nurse's relationship with the patient would change from platonic to romantic. It was interesting to see how, when a nurse became a lover, she cared for the patient and served out of love, not needing a task list to remind her of what her beloved needed. The endurance and skill among these nurses who had fallen in love with their patients was astounding. They would work much harder when they were in love with the patient than they ever did when it was just part of their job. My point is that love is a much better motivator than duty. Love changes the way we respond to the needs (or will) of another.

And so it is if you are to have a relationship with God. There must be a paradigm shift in your thinking of Him as an eternal lover if you are to become a lover of God. Becoming a lover of God will transform how you live for Him.

THE LONGINGS OF THE HUMAN HEART

Within every human heart are deep cravings that cannot be ignored or denied—they must be satisfied. In more than thirty years of ministry, I have been a student of how human emotions work and influence our life choices and decisions. I have enjoyed listening to people talk about what excites them. I have watched thousands of people come through our spiritual community here at the International House of Prayer in Kansas City (IHOP-KC). Some visitors were internationally known teachers with fifty years of ministry experience, while others were eighteen-year-old interns. They have come from a broad variety of church—and unchurched—backgrounds. Some have large budgets, and others are poor. They come with big moving trucks or with everything they own crammed in a backpack. While no two are quite alike, what I have found most interesting is that all people have a common bond: a feeling of longing. A longing is not merely a need for which we can demand satisfaction. Longing goes deeper than that. A longing is an ache of the heart.

The idea of longing spans the gap between emotion and genuine need. It is a feeling that ebbs and flows, and yet it is a concrete reality. It cannot be reasoned with, negated, or dismissed. If not attended to, it will overtake us. A longing will be filled one way or the other.

These longings give us understanding into the way that God designed our spirit. These cravings built into our design reveal the genius of God as our Creator. He strategically put these longings in us as a reflection of His own personality. Deep within our hearts, He intentionally placed these longings there to woo us into His grace and presence. While our first reaction may be to fight against these natural longings, as we begin to identify their origins in God, we open a door to cooperating with them in accordance with His will. We find the answer to our longings in the One who put them in us.

I have outlined a series of seven longings that are universal to every human heart. These seven longings that we have draw us to God and reflect His glory in us. They are the longing:

1. For the assurance that we are enjoyed by God
2. To be fascinated
3. For beauty
4. To be great
5. For intimacy without shame
6. To be wholehearted and passionate
7. To make a deep and lasting impact

When we understand the longings that He created within us, then we understand our struggle and the purposes of life better. When these longings are not touched in the grace of God, they leave us empty; they leave us with pain, mourning, and dissatisfaction.

These longings are actually expressions of His image. We feel delight because He feels delight. We experience joy because He is joy. Our longings are fulfilled in experiencing who He is and in walking out who He created us to become in His image. These "designer cravings" are an essential part of His beauty in our lives. Let's look at each of these seven longings, beginning with the first: the longing to know that God enjoys us.

1. The longing to know that God enjoys us

The greatest need within our soul and spirit is the longing to know that God enjoys us, that He delights in us. We long to know that God the Father enjoys our company and takes pleasure in being with us. The closest earthly example that I can give you is the parent/child relationship. Girls especially are usually very close to their fathers. From the time she is born, a little girl yearns to know that she has her father's undivided attention—24/7—and that he delights in her. She wants to know that she is the apple of her father's eye. She will do whatever it takes to grab his attention and keep it.

Each of us longs to know that God the Father enjoys us, even if we do not recognize that characteristic for what it is. Within each of us is a desire to fill the void these longings create until they are satisfied in the grace of God. Granted, they may not be fully met in this lifetime, but even a little touch of God goes along way. To encounter God in these areas describes being fully alive.

The church must come to the realization that one cannot repent their way out of these longings of the heart but only out of seeking to fulfill them in wrong ways. We cannot repent of the way God spiritually formed us any more than we can repent of our physical DNA. No one has ever thought of asking God's forgiveness for being tall or having brown eyes. People may or may not like these individual characteristics, but they do not view them as wrong; they have learned to accept the fact that these physical traits are just a part of who they are. So it is with these longings of the heart. These longings are as much a part of who you are as the color of your eyes. When you learn to embrace them in a healthy, godly way, allowing God to answer them with Himself, the only true satisfaction, then you will begin to really touch the superior pleasures of the gospel and enter into the joyous realm of living for which we were created.

The Puritans had the tendency to view all pleasure as sinful. Thus, even today…if something is enjoyable, it is sometimes viewed with suspicion and disdain. How could it be godly and enjoyable at the same time? One of our IHOP-KC intercessory missionaries remembers his Bible college professor explaining how he was raised believing that anything that was pleasurable was sinful. Because of this, during his childhood he was never allowed to play any sport that involved a ball. The professor explained it this way: "Daddy wouldn't let us play basketball or baseball. We'd always ask him how he knew those things were a sin, and he'd tell us, 'If it's round, it's wrong!'"

Most of the church has left that type of thinking behind, but we have retained the essence of belief that anything that gives us pleasure is somehow wrong and must be squashed. The result is a church full of people with genuine, God-given longings, lecturing one another on why it's wrong to feel the way they do. Meanwhile, God cries out to them, "I made you that way!"

We cannot repent our way out of these longings; we can only satisfy them in the gospel. The great tension of life is seen in our temptation to satisfy these seven longings outside of the gospel. The Lord wants us to repent of seeking to fulfill them in unsanctified ways. To fulfill them in a right way will make us powerful in our hearts as we resist pride, covetousness, pornography, the occult, bitterness, rage, and so on. We are not to live powerless and hopeless lives. These seven longings of the human spirit must be answered if we are going to walk in the kind of resiliency needed before the onslaught of temptation and rage that Satan is about to vomit out of hell.

The enemy uses these cravings to woo us into darkness as well. Unable to deny their longings, many people attempt to fulfill them outside of the gospel. Of course, Satan is more than accommodating in this endeavor. Because Satan is master of the counterfeit, each longing finds a counterfeit fulfillment in our fallen state.

Why did God place these longings within us? Surely He knew we would run around in search of them, finding only temporary relief in counterfeit answers. But when we gain an understanding of the nature of these seven longings and God's desire to fulfill them in our lives, then we view our purpose in life in a whole new way.

2. The longing to be fascinated

We have an intense longing to be fascinated. Without being fascinated, we live bored, disillusioned, and cynical lives. The secular entertainment industry seeks to exploit this longing of fascination. When we are spiritually bored in our relationship with Jesus, we become much more vulnerable to Satan's attacks.

We crave the exhilaration that fascination brings. God formed this yearning in us so that He could answer by revealing Himself to us. Paul said, "Things which eye has not seen and ear has not heard, and which have not entered into the heart of man, all that God has prepared for those who love Him" (1 Cor. 2:9). Our highest imaginings cannot perceive the fullness of God's beauty and glory. He will cause us to be awestruck over and over throughout the eternal ages.

Most of the Western church today is not fascinated with God. Consequentially, they can easily become spiritually bored and, therefore, spiritually weak. A spiritually bored church is spiritually boring to the lost. I am encouraged knowing that the Holy Spirit will anoint the church to cry out to Jesus, "Come" (Rev. 22:17). Yes, the church will function as a mature bride that is without spot or blemish (Eph. 5:27). The Holy Spirit will cause the superficiality of the Western church to be totally reversed before Jesus returns. The Holy Spirit will enable us to experience the deep things of God, as the apostle Paul taught, "The Spirit searches all things, even the deep things of God" to reveal them to us (1 Cor. 2:10, NIV). Seeking to grow in the knowledge of God will lead us to a life of being fascinated.

The subject of the knowledge of God is the "Mount Everest of the Christian walk." It is the highest and hardest mountain to climb. In fact, we will be climbing this mountain for all of eternity. We will never exhaust the vast ocean of the knowledge of God. One billion years from now, we will still be focused on this subject. What better time to start than now?

The more of the knowledge of God that I receive, the more I understand how spiritually shallow I really am, even when I have energetically pursued the Lord for more than thirty-five years. In the first five years of my journey, I thought I was spiritually deep. Today, I know I am merely on the sandy beach of the ocean of God's

Being, with the waves of revelation barely washing up over my feet. I look forward to exploring the depths of this ocean throughout eternity.

I compare our journey into the depths of God to a man who is advanced in mathematics. For example, think of a man working on his master's thesis at Harvard University. At that time of his education, he may be confident that he understands math. He may even envision himself as a master of his science. Let's say that as the years progress he becomes a chief mathematician at Houston Control (Johnson Space Center). After forty years of working in the space program, ask him how much math he knows. At that time he will be aware of the possibilities of how much math there is to know in context to the hundred million galaxies in the known universe. (The Milky Way galaxy is one of the smaller galaxies in the known universe.) It is then that he best knows how much math he does not know and how much he has yet to learn in his field. In other words, the more of God we experience, the more we become aware of how much we do not know.

3. *The longing for beauty*

The primary occupation of David's life, the chief drive of his heart, was to encounter God's beauty. In this, he was one of the most unique kings in history. Psalm 27:4 is one of the International House of Prayer's foundational scriptures and has been one of my favorites for a long time:

> One thing I have desired of the LORD,
> That will I seek:
> That I may dwell in the house of the LORD
> All the days of my life,
> To behold the beauty of the LORD,
> And to inquire in His temple.
>
> —PSALM 27:4, NKJV

Most people grasp the idea that David was a man after God's own heart, but they lose themselves in a catchphrase mentality when looking at this psalm. David desired to seek one thing all of his life: to behold or to experience the beauty of God. This statement is more radical than it could at first appear to be. David is not exaggerating or being hyperbolic in this statement. David's responsibilities included leading one of the most powerful nations in the world at that time, as well as being the commander in chief of Israel's military forces. Even with these two massive responsibilities, David claimed that his primary focus in life was to gaze on God's beauty. As a man after God's heart, David was a student of God's emotions. He did not merely obey God's heart, but he also studied God's heart. He wanted to know what God's heart was like.

No other king has exhibited this single-minded drive to base his life primarily on encountering God's beauty. We could call it David's glorious obsession. He is an amazing picture of a man living fascinated with God. David wrote that he sought God's beauty "all the days" of his life. That included his boyhood days as a shepherd and his time as a fugitive running for his life as King Saul chased him through the wilderness of Israel. This pursuit continued until the time of his death at seventy years of age. We are also invited by the Spirit to live in this same fascination with God's beauty on a daily basis throughout our lives both now and for all eternity.

One of the most profound promises for God's people in the End Times is found in Isaiah 4:2. In this verse, God promises to strike the human heart with awe as He reveals His Son to them. Isaiah prophesied, "In that day the Branch of the LORD [Jesus] will be beautiful and glorious." We shall be fully engrossed in Jesus' beauty and glory when the Holy Spirit takes the things of Jesus and imparts them to us (John 16:14). God will reveal God to our human spirits, causing us to be exhilarated. This lifetime of experiences will be unlike any other; it will be greater than any physical or emotional pleasure that we know.

Again, Isaiah promises us that our "eyes will see the King in His beauty" (Isa. 33:17). This amazing prophecy is to be read together with Isaiah 4:2 to give us the full picture of the revelation that we are to receive. Not only is Jesus beautiful beyond comprehension, but also there is a day coming when we shall see Him. A lifetime of longing will be suddenly answered as we gaze upon our Maker and Redeemer. We will never grow bored gazing upon Him. If the fiery seraphim do not, how could we? What begins in initial fascination will continue to grow. What all the striving of mankind could not attain, God will do in fullness for all eternity—He will truly fascinate our hearts. He will put Himself on display—the essence of beauty, the perfection of splendor and magnificence. Jesus' name is called "Wonderful" in Isaiah 9:6 because He alone can fill the heart of His people with wonder. "He is Wonderful" will be the confession of the redeemed. The saints on the sea of glass in heaven will forever marvel at Jesus (Rev. 15:2).

4. The longing to be great

The longing for greatness is the universal desire to be an integral part of something bigger than ourselves. The longing to be great involves succeeding or prospering in being promoted to positions of meaningful influence, honor, authority, or importance.

Everyone chooses the story to which they belong, and then they seek to find their place within it. Whatever you choose to derive the meaning of your life from determines what the goal of greatness looks like for the individual. That is why greatness for an athlete and greatness for a scientist look so drastically different—the longing is the same, but the application is disparate.

Solomon, one of King David's sons and ultimately heir to the throne, longed to be great among God's people, Israel. But it was not a longing to be a great leader for the sake of greatness; it was a longing to rule God's people with wisdom because Solomon feared God and longed to please Him. Like his father before him, initially, Solomon's heart delighted in doing what pleased God.

It was God who established David's throne, and it was Solomon whom God had chosen to perpetuate it. Solomon was just a child when he was called to sit on the throne (1 Kings 3:7), and he recognized that he was too immature to lead a nation. The night that God appeared to Solomon, God told him to ask for whatever he wanted, and the only things Solomon asked for were wisdom and knowledge to be a great leader (2 Chron. 1:10). At a young age, Solomon heeded his father's words of wisdom, and he knew in his young, tender heart that the "fear of the LORD is the beginning of wisdom" and that knowledge of Him would add years to his life (Prov. 9:10–11). God blessed Solomon not only with wisdom and knowledge, making him the wisest man ever, but also with riches and honor. He also promised Solomon long life as long as he obeyed God's laws as his father, David, had done (1 Kings 3:14). David obeyed God because he was passionate about knowing Him. Solomon obeyed God because he longed to please God.

Affection-based obedience is the most effective way to live a life of holiness or passion for Jesus. Some Christians have been like the self-assured Pharaoh who asked Moses, "Who is the LORD that I should obey His voice?" (Exod. 5:2). Directly or indirectly, many believers have asked a similar question: "Who is Jesus Christ that He should command total obedience from His people?" As a result, the awakening church is now looking around in despair, surveying the wreckage resulting from her ignorance of God's personhood, her lack of discipleship, and her partial obedience. Years of passivity and careless compromise have taken a great toll. For ages, the church has talked about the price of obedience; now she is learning the dreadful price of disobedience.

When we understand the affection that God has for us, it awakens our affection back to Him. This is the most powerful and effective source to sustain a life of holiness and obedience to God. Affection is unique to human beings; there is nothing in Scripture about angels having affection. They have joy and other emotions, but those are not affection. Only human beings have been given the dignity of possessing the burning desire of affectionate love. God gave us this privilege so that we might voluntarily choose Him in love with all of our heart, soul, mind, and strength.

A life characterized by affection-based obedience is a life in which you are so loved, and so love God, that obedience is the only reasonable response to anything He wishes. For the sake of love, you are willing to give everything and find no sacrifice too great.

5. *The longing for intimacy without shame*

Let's be clear about this: Satan did not come up with the idea of pleasure. The realm of pleasure belongs squarely in God's camp. Satan, however, counterfeited it and destroyed the heart of humanity by offering what was not real. The reason people find themselves disappointed with what Satan has to offer is that what he offers will never truly satisfy them.

God has granted the human design physical pleasures, emotional pleasures, and mental pleasures, but the most profound pleasures are spiritual in nature. They are made evident when God the Holy Spirit reveals God the Son to the human spirit.

The superior pleasures of the gospel are implied in Matthew 22:2. When Jesus referred to the kingdom as a bridegroom and bride at a wedding, He was pointing to a whole new door of experience in redemption—the experience of being a cherished bride.

Tragically, the inferior pleasures of sin have the potential to dominate our lives if they are the only pleasures that we experience. If someone lives in a vacuum of experience with God—having little knowledge or experience of who He is—then the inferior pleasures of sin will offer us a counterfeit, limited fulfillment.

Many Christians focus only on resisting the inferior pleasures that Satan offers. They look at their sin and promise God, "I'll never, ever do that again!" They make promises and go through religious incantations, always seeking to be set free. Still, in the back of their mind, they are remembering that sin was pleasurable. It was wrong, but it felt good. It was sin, but it was all the pleasure they have ever known. They struggle to live their lives in Christ, but if they were honest, they would have to admit that the days before they knew Jesus were the "good ol' days."

God's desire is to shock us with the pleasures that are available in relationship with Him. He taps us on the shoulder and whispers, "Turn around...look at the superior pleasures, the beauty of My Son, the greatness of who you are in God—My chosen partner who will rule and reign with Me forever and ever!"

When we fix our gaze on these things—the greater pleasures of God—something happens in our heart. The first commandment shifts into first place, and we begin to live for Him wholeheartedly. The pleasures that sin had to offer suddenly appear as they really are—cold and hollow. Covetousness, pornography, and bitterness are not nearly as powerful when you are brushing up against the superior pleasures of God and touching the vast enjoyment therein. When the scales are removed from our eyes, we realize just how much God has to offer—and how what He has to offer is precisely what we have been pursuing.

6. The longing to be wholehearted and passionate

You can always identify a couple that is newly wedded because of their passion and wholehearted commitment to one another. There is a longing to be together every possible moment of the day.

They give themselves to each other wholeheartedly, without any reservation.

When the church returns to her first love, then she will discover a fascination with her Bridegroom. The longing we have to wholeheartedly be with Him will be satisfied. The beauty of Jesus reaches its height in the paradigm of a Messiah who is not only our King but also our Bridegroom God. Jesus is our Bridegroom King. This is the revelation of Jesus by which the End-Time church will be ravished. We will suffer every kind of persecution and undergo every form of tribulation, yet remain fervent in love. We will give our lives even unto death with eyes fixed unwavering upon our Bridegroom.

The Holy Spirit is giving the church a deeper revelation of Jesus' beauty to answer our craving for awe and wonder. The revelation of Jesus to our hearts will liberate us from the soul-sapping inferior pleasures of sin by introducing us to superior pleasures of knowing Jesus. Sin loses its domination in the lives of those fascinated with Christ Jesus. A fascinated man does not need pornography, alcohol, mindless entertainment, or any other sedatives to make his life work. God has a better strategy than simply forcing us to grit our teeth and struggle in the quicksand mire of evil. God will release a new anointing on the church worldwide. Perceiving Jesus' beauty will result in a supernatural strengthening of the inner man. Within the bridal paradigm God will answer our craving for awe and wonder by revealing to us the beauty of the Bridegroom (Ps. 45:2).

7. The longing to make a deep and lasting impact

When we started IHOP-KC on May 7, 1999, we had no idea that four months later—on September 19, 1999—we would begin our twenty-four-hour-a-day prayer schedule. Here in Kansas City, Missouri, we presently have eighty-four two-hour prayer meetings each week. Each worship team is comprised of ten to twelve people, including the singers. We have several hundred staff members who have raised their own financial support as they function as "intercessory missionaries" committed to the Great Commission (Matt. 28:19). The Lord has been good to us in helping to maintain this ministry without stopping. The IHOP-KC staff is committed to keep the fire of prayer burning on God's altar, not allowing it to go out (Lev. 6:12–13).

We have hundreds of visitors to IHOP-KC each week. They come from many different nations. The most common question that we are asked by our visitors is how to do 24/7 prayer and worship in their city. Some are expecting us to answer by giving them administrative details on our structure. However, the key issue to sustaining 24/7 prayer and worship is to raise up singers and musicians who are fascinated with God's beauty. I do not pretend that the IHOP-KC staff is at the pinnacle of revelatory fascination, sitting in starry-eyed, mesmerized delight of God. If you ask them, they will tell you that they sometimes experience dryness in prayer and that they struggle in their spiritual lives just as everyone else does. However, when God the Holy Spirit reveals God the Father and God the Son to our hearts, we become fascinated, and we are left with the greatest pleasure available to our human experience. This is one of the greatest promises that the church has, and without it, 24/7 prayer and worship is impossible, and spiritual boredom will always set in. In the coming years, I am confident God will do this same thing in other cities around the earth.

MOTIVATED TO FASCINATION WITH THE BRIDEGROOM

The master plan of God is an amazing thing…to create a bride for His Son, watch her fall into imperfection, and then offer His Son to redeem the bride for Himself. All along, God rests in the confidence of knowing that from the dawn of creation He had endowed that bride with longings she could never ignore. He knew that the enemy would use those longings to manipulate Jesus' bride. Even this did not make God nervous. He knew what He had to offer. As she ran from place to place trying to fulfill those longings, God was patiently sure that she would only find fulfillment in returning to the task she was created for—to be the bride of Christ. She had to come home if she was ever to be truly happy. God will unlock the heart of His people; He is going to bring us into the superior pleasures of the gospel. He is going to cause us to know obedience rooted in lovesickness. My premise is that the bridal paradigm is the most powerful gospel truth that transforms our hearts to empower us to love. This paradigm has the most powerful impact on our emotional chemistry.

My premise is that the Holy Spirit will use this bridal paradigm to motivate us to extravagant obedience more powerfully than any other paradigm found in the Word of God. The Great Commission will not be fulfilled without martyrs. Many ministries in the coming hour will be sufficiently anointed to equip "joyful martyrs" even in the Western church. Worldwide, there were more martyrs in the twentieth century than at any other time in history.[1] Until now, the Western church has been exempt for the most part. This will soon change. The apostle John related a vision that he had that reveals the prominent role of the martyrs in the last days:

> When He opened the fifth seal, I saw under the altar the souls of those who had been slain for the word of God and for the testimony which they held. And they cried with a loud voice, saying, "How long, O Lord, holy and true, until You judge and avenge our blood on those who dwell on the earth?" Then a white robe was given to each of them; and it was said to them that they should rest a little while longer, until both the number of their

fellow servants and their brethren, who would be killed as they
were, was completed.

—REVELATION 6:9–11, NKJV

How will these martyrs be empowered? They will experience
a deep spiritual intimacy with Jesus. This intimacy results from
feasting on the knowledge of the beauty and majesty of Jesus, the
Bridegroom King. These martyrs will abundantly experience the
superior pleasures of the gospel in contrast to the bridal paradigm
of the kingdom. John describes a victorious multitude of joyful
worshiping martyrs at the end of the age.

And I saw…those who have the victory over the beast…stand-
ing on the sea of glass, having harps of God.

—REVELATION 15:2, NKJV

As we consider these seven longings of the human heart,
begin to look at them as our road map to viewing the Lord as our
Bridegroom and ourselves as His eternal chosen companion. In
order to fulfill these longings, we must see Him as a Bridegroom,
but in order to see Him as our Bridegroom, we must first come to
Him for satisfaction in our longings. There is no way around it. We
will never be satisfied in the false pursuit of temporary fulfillments.
Only when we begin to touch and experience some of these eternal
satisfactions will we be empowered to let go of the inferior. No matter how easy it is to prop up our lives around counterfeit pleasures,
we must give ourselves in wholehearted pursuit to the pleasures
that will continue to carry us even billions of years from now. Yes,
Jesus is coming back for a church filled with passion for Jesus.

CHAPTER 5

FROM INTIMATE KNOWLEDGE TO PASSIONATE LOVE

I walked into the little storefront room to speak to a group of new Christians, never dreaming that my life was about to be changed forever. I was twenty-one years old and pastoring a small country church. My eyes scanned the little group of Christians who had gathered in the room. It was then that I noticed the beautiful, young, blonde girl across the room. I flipped out! I had never felt such intense emotions as I gazed across the room at Diane, the girl who was to become my wife.

My love for Diane and my desire to be with her helped me understand the love Christ felt for His bride. His prayer in John 17 especially moved me: "Father, I desire that they also, whom Thou hast given Me, be with Me where I am" (John 17:24). Here was my Lord, only hours before His agonizing death at Calvary, crying out to the Father with intense cravings for His bride—for me!

He was consumed with love for His bride and longed to have His bride with Him for eternity.

THE FOUR PROPHETIC STATEMENTS IN JESUS' PRAYER

I took a fresh look at this high priestly prayer, which, I believe, is one of the most significant intercessory prayers in all of Scripture.

Toward the end of this prayer, Jesus' focus changes from the first generation of Christians to the church throughout history. He intercedes for believers who will come to know Him after His death. We find prophetic promises for the church in this prayer.

Once we go beyond a superficial reading of John 17:20–26, we begin to see that every phrase contains deep meaning. At the end of this prophetic prayer Jesus gave us a glimpse of the powerful and passionate church He would build:

> I have declared to them Your name, and will declare it, that the love with which You loved Me may be in them, and I in them.
>
> —JOHN 17:26, NKJV

How magnificent it is to see the Son of God praying for the church, His beloved bride, one last time while He is still clothed in human flesh. Jesus' prayer for such a church to love Him as the Father loves Him will undoubtedly be answered. It was directed by the Father, energized by the Holy Spirit, and prayed in accordance with the Father's will. Jesus never prayed amiss.

Obviously this prayer contains an eternal dimension, but verses 21–23 reveal that the answer to this prayer lies not just in heaven. It will come to pass on this side of eternity so the unsaved can witness it. Jesus prayed that the world would behold such a church. The beginnings of its fulfillment lie in this age.

In verse 26 we find four key phrases describing Christ's earthly ministry. Let's look at these phrases one at a time, examining them more closely.

1. "I have declared to them Your name"

"I have declared to them Your name." That was the consuming purpose beating in the heart of Jesus during His three and a half years of earthly ministry. When it was all over, He summed up His entire earthly ministry by saying to His Father, "I've made Your name known to them." In other words, Jesus had given the people a revelation of the knowledge of God and let them know what His Father was like. He made known to them the splendor of His Father's personality.

I do not think Jesus Christ enjoys anything more than revealing to others the infinite splendor and awesome beauty of His Father. Every aspect of His ministry reflects the indescribable loveliness of the Father. Here, at the end of His life on earth, Jesus' great claim is that He has made the Father known to the people.

We sometimes talk about the ministry of Jesus only in terms of physical and emotional healing or the preaching of forgiveness. But the ministry of Jesus was not confined just to miracles and forgiveness. Both of these categories of Christ's ministry support the greater element of His mission on this earth. The ministry of Jesus was most significantly defined by His making known the splendor of His Father.

When people heard Jesus' words, observed His lifestyle, and beheld His perfectly balanced personality and flawless character, they received a glimpse of the beauty of what God the Father is like.

It was Christ's great joy to reveal His Father. You and I have the same privilege and responsibility. Paul reminds us of that fact:

> But thanks be to God, who always leads us in His triumph in Christ, and manifests through us the sweet aroma of the knowledge of Him in every place.
>
> —2 CORINTHIANS 2:14

The Spirit of God leads us into triumph and victory so that we can manifest the sweet aroma of the knowledge of God everywhere we go. I experienced some of this triumph when I learned to release the anger and bitterness I had felt in caring for my injured brother. As I let go of the anger, the Holy Spirit imparted to me a measure of His love along with new insight into God's heart. God desires that we experience fellowship with the Holy Spirit so that we will be transformed—led into victory from the inside out—a victory touching our hearts, minds, and emotions. Then we will manifest a measure of the sweet fragrance of the knowledge of God in private, in public, and in all our casual interactions. That's what Jesus did in fullness.

A sweet aroma is often the manifestation of the presence of God. When we see God in another person, whether in their actions, words, or quiet spirits, a pure freshness touches our hearts. Every time the Spirit of God enables us to break a bondage or to triumph over an addiction or weakness and come into victory, that conquest releases in us more of the fragrance of our glorious Father (2 Cor. 2:14).

Jesus described His ministry as making His Father's name known to others. My goal is to help people think of ministry as more than something that happens in meetings or when we serve, counsel, or pray for others. *Ministry* at its most basic definition is "the manifestation of the knowledge of God through our lives."

The invisible aroma of the knowledge of God that the apostle Paul talked about has power. It lifts us from one degree of life to another. Our hearts become softer and more tender. We grow more caring, compassionate, patient, and forgiving. We become more sensitive to the Spirit of God. We are more like Jesus. In order to grow into maturity, we must know God the Father more intimately. Our most vital ministry is revealing the beauty of God's personality to others.

It's easy to read a book or listen to a tape, memorizing new truths to talk about. It's easy to be an echo of truth instead of a voice that resonates with the truth. There is a certain quality of ministry that comes only as you and I touch God in reality in our secret lives.

To be mature Christians, each one of us must have a secret life in

God hidden from the eyes of others. I remember the early days of my journey of becoming more intimate with God. I would come before Him with a list of needs and wants. I struggled to feel His presence as I tossed my words into the air, rarely experiencing His presence.

I recall the day that I was in my office praying. I had finished reading the Song of Solomon and praying the invitation of Jesus to set Him as a seal on my heart: "Set me as a seal upon your heart…for love is strong as death. Its flames are flames of fire" (Song of Sol. 8:6, NKJV). I was overwhelmed with God's presence. He was softening my heart at that moment. Tears flowed down my face. Not wanting to lose the preciousness of the moment, I quietly called my receptionist and asked her to make sure that no one interrupted me for the next thirty minutes.

I had been worshiping at His feet for about fifteen minutes when my secretary suddenly rang into my office saying, "I'm sorry, but the caller says it is very important that he speak to you right away."

Annoyed at being distracted, I picked up the phone. An acquaintance of mine was on the other end of the line. "Mike," he began excitedly, "I had a prophetic dream about you last night. The Lord has clearly shown me that I am to give a particular Bible verse to you. It is Song of Solomon 8:6." My annoyance left as I listened to his words: "God says that you are to set Him as a seal upon your heart. He wanted you to know that right now."

In this encounter with the Lord, the Holy Spirit was revealing God's heart and passion for me. I long to proclaim with Jesus, "Father, I have declared to them Your name."

2. "…*and will declare it*"

In the next breath Jesus made a glorious statement pertaining to the future: "…and [I] will declare [Your name]." Jesus knew that after His resurrection, when He was seated at His Father's right hand, He would continue to reveal the majestic heart of the Father through the ministry of the Holy Spirit moving through the church. His priority would be to continue revealing the Father's name or His passions, desires, and pleasures to and through His church.

Before Jesus comes *for* the church at the Second Coming, He will come *to* the church in revelation and power. Paul said that the church will come to "the knowledge of the Son of God" (Eph. 4:13). His indescribable loveliness will be revealed to His people in a far greater measure in the great revival before His Second Coming. The church will be filled with the intimate knowledge of God the Father and the Son by the power and revelation of the Holy Spirit.

Jesus' passion is to continue to reveal the Father. That's what He is doing now in His heavenly ministry at the right hand of the Father. That is what He will do through all eternity. The church today must be in agreement with this present ministry of Jesus— revealing the Father to people's hearts. Those who deeply encounter the ministry of the resurrected Christ will be captured by the beauty and splendor of the Father's name and personality.

3. "…that the love with which You loved Me may be in them"

"I have declared to them Your name, and will declare it." Why? "That the love with which You loved Me may be in them." When Jesus reveals the Father's heart to us, or when we "see God" in a greater way, then the Father's love for Jesus is imparted to our hearts. Imagine the massive implications of this. Jesus taught us in this passage that what we see affects how we feel. In other words, our emotions are changed and love is imparted to us to the degree that we see God's splendor or encounter His name.

Jesus is praying that the body of Christ will love Him the way the Father loves Him. This is an awesome prayer. Jesus will reveal the Father, and in turn, the Father will capture our hearts for the Son. Jesus' prayer probably goes something like this:

> Father, You are so infinitely beautiful. Your splendor is beyond their understanding. I want to make You known. I know You will capture the hearts of the people for Me. They will feel for Me as You feel for Me. My beloved bride, My eternal companion, the one You ordained to rule with Me as a coheir, will love Me as You love Me.

Here we can see some of the dynamic cooperation at work within the Godhead. God the Father desires a people who love Jesus as He does. A people who see and feel what God sees and feels when He looks at His beloved Son. God will have *a passionate church* that loves Jesus as God loves Him.

The Father chose Jesus' bride for Him and has ordained that she have the very extravagant passion for His beloved Son that He has.

Yes, the church will be filled with many different activities and ministries, but the single most distinctive issue in the Father's heart is to capture the church with passionate affections for His dear Son. The Holy Spirit is zealous to accomplish that purpose in this hour. In today's fast-lane living it's easy to allow ourselves to lose focus on loving Jesus in the midst of a full day at the office, family responsibilities, and many church activities. As William Wordsworth wrote almost two hundred years ago, "The world is too much with us…Getting and spending, we lay waste our powers."[1] In all of our getting, we must acquire passion for God.

I have to remind myself that I am not called to be a spiritual politician that needs to be at every church activity. I am called to be a man filled with holy passion and affection for Jesus. That is what I want to minister to people. I have chosen as the ultimate purpose of my life to know the Father's name and to make it known. In other words, to love Jesus in the way the Father loves Him and to inspire others to this quality of intimacy with God.

4. "...and I in them"

First, Jesus said, "I have declared to them Your name." Then He said, "I will declare it." Why? So that the same love the Father has for Jesus would fill our hearts. Now Jesus states the fourth principle: "I will be in them."

As the riches of the knowledge of God are revealed, what is the result? The quality of love the Father has for the Son will be in the church. Jesus will dwell in His people; that is, He will manifest His supernatural life in and through them.

The cycle goes all the way around. When Jesus manifests His life's ministry through us, we declare God's name and make Him known to others. Then we are, in turn, awakened with passion for Jesus, leading to lifestyles characterized by His presence.

Every prayer of Jesus was a prophetic promise. Every time He prayed it was according to the will of His Father. This prayer of Jesus Christ in John 17 will be answered. It's a wonderful, prophetic promise for the church!

A REVIVAL OF INTIMACY AND PASSION

It takes the power of God to make God known to the human spirit. This knowledge enables us to love God. As I said earlier, it takes God to love God, and it takes God to know God.

The church will be filled with the knowledge of God. Jesus said it. His promises never fail. The Holy Spirit will use the release of this knowledge to awaken a deep intimacy with Jesus. A revival of the knowledge of God is coming, and as a result the church will be filled with holy passion for Jesus. Divinely imparted passion for Jesus is on the Holy Spirit's agenda as seen in Jesus' prayer.

Obviously, this prophetic prayer for the church has not been totally fulfilled yet. It is sadly apparent that today's church does not love Jesus as the Father does. Furthermore, we can find no place in history where that prayer has been fulfilled in any major worldwide way. However, we know that the Father Himself is committed to answering this prayer. The heart of the Lord will be known by His people, and the church will love Jesus as God the Father loves His Son, Jesus.

HOW SHALL THESE THINGS BE?

My heart is grieved over the increasing immorality in our society. Immorality has reached an all-time high. It pains me to know that pornography, prostitution, and nudity have become so rampant in many international cities today. The world is consumed with counterfeit passion.

I believe that the generation in which the Lord returns will be filled with emotional brokenness to a level unprecedented in human history. The perversion and woundedness of the human heart will reach unimagined proportions. Sinful perversion, occult activity, divine judgment, and widespread martyrdom will reach a level of intensity that man has never known. The pornography industry will continue to intersect with rapidly growing technology. The same will happen with the occult.

Jesus described the last generation as being filled with bitterness, offense, and betrayal, with their hearts growing cold in love (Matt. 24:10–14). In this dark and pressing time, God has strategically reserved the revelation of the church as Jesus' cherished bride (Eph. 5:25–32) as His answer to the unique and complex pressures of the generation when the Lord returns. It is God-inspired to empower the church to overcome the coldest, most lawless, fearful, demonic, and sexually perverted generation in history.

I have looked at the lukewarm, compromising church of our day and wondered, *How shall these things be? Will such a glorious revival really come to pass?* Then I remember Israel's negative spiritual condition during the time of Jesus' earthly ministry. The church's only hope is that God is rich in mercy. Therefore, at His appointed time, God will supernaturally intervene. The same flaming zeal in the heart of the Father that compelled Him to send Jesus the first time will manifest as He revives the compromising church in this generation. The zeal of the Lord of hosts shall perform it.

The only way we will overcome sinful passions is by replacing them with holy passions. It will not happen because we are better than other generations. Such passion always comes from encountering God's name or personality because of Jesus' work on the cross.

There is nothing Jesus wants more than a bride who loves what He loves and does what He does. He longs for a bride who will participate in the passions and purposes of His heart. Jesus will have an eternal companion filled with holy affection for Him. We long to be a part of a glorious, spotless church in our generation—a church filled with the knowledge of God, reflecting His glory and consumed with passion for Jesus. Such a church will be prepared to engage in the great conflict that is to come.

Jesus is going to cleanse His church, washing us with the Word and presenting us to Himself as something more glorious than we can imagine. Paul described it this way: "That He [Jesus] might...cleanse her [the church] with the washing of water by the word, that He might present her to Himself a glorious church, not having spot or wrinkle or any such thing, but that she should be holy and without blemish" (Eph. 5:26–27, NKJV).

When the Word refers to us as having no spot or wrinkle, it is not merely speaking of our legal standing of justification. Obviously we will stand blameless because He died for us. This refers to actual character worked into the heart of the people of God. This will happen without violating our free will. In other words, we will fully cooperate with the process.

This washing and being presented to Christ can only be accomplished in the context of the church as a bride. He is not said to be washing a family, an army, or a farmer—He washes *His bride*.

Before the return of the Lord, the church will have a fierce and determined spirituality based in affection for God. I believe that passion for Jesus with extravagant obedience will be the norm among believers across the globe. It takes the Spirit of God to love God. We need the Spirit's impartation of God's love to equip us to love God. Our desire for God is God's gift to us. Our love and desire for God are expressions of His desire for us.

All the emotional resources necessary for His people to walk victoriously in love will flow out of our enjoyment of God as we walk in our bridal identity. To the human spirit, sin appears to be the most pleasurable thing we can experience until we experience the true romance of the gospel. Then as the Spirit of God reveals God to us, the Lord escorts us into experiencing the superior pleasures of the gospel.

CHAPTER 6

ESCORTED INTO THE BEAUTY OF GOD

As we grow in passionate love for Jesus, it becomes a natural reaction to want to live fascinated with His beauty. Just as the maiden in Song of Solomon 3:1–4 seeks her lover, so Jesus leaves and then allows Himself to be found.

God is like the father who plays hide-and-seek with his child. Each time they play, the father hides behind the only tree in the yard, peering around it with twinkling eyes, a huge smile on his face, and stretching out one leg so that his child is sure to find him. Like that father, God hides Himself in a way that He can be found, but His desire is that we walk with the Holy Spirit and allow Him to escort us deeper and deeper into the wonder of His infinite beauty. But how are we to establish the practical beginnings of such a lifelong journey?

Memorizing the works of the scholarly masters is no substitute, and reading through a library of the most enlightened inspired manuscripts will impart nothing if the Holy Spirit is not involved. Reading this book will not cause the beauty of God to take root in your heart. It is the Holy Spirit who searches the deep things of God and reveals them to us (1 Cor. 2:10). Without His participation, studying the beauty of God will remain a cold fact, and the experience that I have urged you to explore will not come.

God gives us His Holy Spirit so that we can share in the revelation of the deep things of God's heart. We cannot comprehend the realm of God's beauty without the Holy Spirit. Living in close fellowship with the Holy Spirit is an essential part of receiving more revelation.

John was in contact with the Holy Spirit when he experienced the visions in the Book of Revelation. In the same way, God will release His revelation to us by the Person of the Holy Spirit. John's use of the term "in the Spirit" applies to the principle that he had to live in contact with the Spirit as a prerequisite to receive the revelation that God desired to grant him. We must also live in this contact with the Holy Spirit.

In Psalm 15:1, David ponders the question, "Who may abide in Your tabernacle?" (NKJV). The tabernacle is the very home of God. "Who may dwell in Your holy hill?" Again, the question being asked is how to experience intimate closeness to God's holy presence. David repeats the question again in Psalm 24, asking who can stand before a holy God. In Psalm 65:4, David exclaims that the person whom God has chosen to approach Him is blessed.

The most practical application of these psalms in everyday life speaks of the person who eagerly obeys the Holy Spirit as the way to experience God's presence. Scripture emphasizes the importance of being led by the Spirit as the way of encountering God (Gal. 5:18; Rom. 8:14).

The price we pay and the costly choices we make to walk in the beauty of holiness are not noticed or valued by men, but every godly choice we make is precious to God, releasing God's beauty into our hearts. The more we understand how dear this is to God, the more it motivates us to passionately seek Him.

A HIGHER STANDARD

As we increase in our personal walk with the Spirit, He raises the standards of obedience that He requires of us. The more His light illuminates our hearts, the more darkness is revealed in us. The greater the encounter we have with God, the greater the accountability we have before Him.

It is people who seek purity who will see or experience God's presence (Matt. 5:8). The size of our ministry or scope of our influence does not necessarily reflect the size of our hearts, nor is it the basis of our relationship with God or our reward in eternity. Few are called by God to host huge evangelism campaigns or preach before thousands of eager listeners. According to Hebrews 12, however, we are called to the pursuit of holiness. There are no escape clauses or exceptions. There is no evading this glorious call. The pursuit of holiness includes obeying God through the difficult and the easy seasons. A large part of holiness is steadfastness in the assignments of God and persevering through the times of difficulty.

One of our Night Watch worship leaders returns time and again to a chorus gleaned from Psalm 51. "You are perfecting me, you have perfected me," she sings. We are considered perfect through Jesus' blood, but at the same time we are constantly being matured and shaped by the Spirit. Habitual sin can creep in through small and subtle areas in our lives, not always through great and awful misdeeds.

When the Holy Spirit brings my attention to an area of my life that needs to be addressed, I can choose to bend to His leadership, or I can choose to wrestle against Him. Willful disobedience lessens our ability to experience the Holy Spirit's presence.

When mountain climbers scale Mount Everest, they cannot afford to grow lax on the last steps of the climb. That section is called the Death Zone. Even descending through it, they dare not pause or become careless. They have accomplished much more than when they were setting out from base camp, and a good deal of the climb is behind them, but the task becomes more difficult and more intense. In the same way, the more we experience God, the more mature we grow, and the more imperative it becomes that we root out the first seedlings of sin and disobedience and cut off compromise at its source.

Through all of this, we must remember that God loves us and is kind to us every step of the way. If, however, we are to experience the realms of His beauty, we must live in agreement with the Spirit. If we want to encounter God and worship Him, we must do it on His terms. Jesus makes it clear that we must worship "in spirit and truth" (John 4:23). When we worship Him in the Spirit, we also have fellowship with the Spirit.

FELLOWSHIPING WITH THE HOLY SPIRIT

The key to experiencing the beauty of God is to become well acquainted with the Escort who will take us there. We must encounter and walk with the Spirit. Too many people focus upon overcoming the flesh by their own efforts alone. As we have discovered, human zeal can take us only so far before we hit a wall of our own weakness, selfishness, and inadequacy. The Lord wants us to redirect our attention from our own selves to His Spirit who dwells within us. We are to be proactive in encountering the Spirit rather than reactive in fighting a losing battle with sin. If we walk in the Spirit, we will not fulfill the lusts of the flesh (Gal. 5:16). It is as simple as that. By walking in the Spirit, saying no to sin becomes considerably easier. Living a lifestyle of communicating and obeying the Spirit means that the warring that Paul describes in Galatians 5:17 will go a lot better for us.

It is easy to spiritualize the term "walking" or "fellowshiping" with the Holy Spirit. It is better not to. Picture yourself literally walking with the Spirit as you would walk with a friend. The Spirit dwells inside of us, and to have a relationship with Him, we must talk to Him. The same principle exists in forming a relationship with the Holy Spirit as with any other person.

This sort of prayer is not a journey of "self discovery." It is a journey of discovering the holy God who has chosen to live within you. Quiet yourself and tell Him, "Thank You, Holy Spirit, for Your presence. I ask You to lead me and guide me." When I talk to God, I have two different ways of going about it. I talk to Him as the God who sits on His throne as seen in Revelation 4. I think of standing on the sea of glass talking to God, with the emerald rainbow around His throne and with the fire of the Holy Spirit upon me. Also, I talk to the Spirit who lives in my spirit, as I picture Him as a bright light living in my spirit. Jesus says, "Out of your innermost man," or the King James says, "Out of your belly the Spirit flows." (See John 7:38.) I quiet myself and gaze into that glorious light, which is God the Holy Spirit living within me. The pictures given in the Book of John and the Book of Revelation are of a flaming light or of a spring of water, and these images can be invaluable when fellowshiping with the Spirit.

I do not say a lot of words, but I simply thank Him for His presence, and I say very simple phrases like, "Release Your strength in me. Strengthen me, Spirit." Or I say, "Lead me, Holy Spirit." Or, "Teach me, Holy Spirit." I quiet my soul and gaze into that glorious light of the Spirit who dwells in me. I pose my heart to gaze on the indwelling Spirit. I am more quiet than talkative. Perhaps every minute or two I say something simple like, "Lead me, Holy Spirit. I love Your leadership." Above all, I listen to what He has to say. He speaks by giving impressions to my heart. If I talk to Him, He will talk back.

After we decide to get involved in the conversation with the Spirit, He will communicate back to us. He speaks to us by giving us subtle impressions that release power on our minds and renewed resolution on our hearts if we respond to them. In this way, friendship with the Spirit is cultivated.

When we begin this fellowship with the Spirit, the resources of the Spirit will become evident in our lives. The fruit of the Spirit is "love, joy, peace, patience ["longsuffering," NKJV], kindness, goodness, faithfulness, gentleness, self-control" (Gal. 5:22–23). The fruit of this well is imparted to us, given to us by the Holy Spirit. It does not come out of some fictitious well of good intentions or positivity that we somehow conjure up within ourselves; the fruit is a direct and infused grace of the Spirit. These infusions strengthen us (Eph. 3:16) as we war against lust as Paul described (Gal. 5:17). Our friendship with the Spirit is what ultimately draws us into the experience of God's beauty, and it is available to all.

Do not become discouraged when you start talking to the Holy Spirit and at first He seems far away. You are promised that your desire will eventually be satisfied (Matt. 5:6). God hides Himself that He might be sought out by those who refuse to live without the deep communion that He promises.

God withdraws His presence at times, not out of cruelty, but to inspire our hunger and stir us to come after Him. It is the glory of God to hide a matter, but the glory of a king to search out the matter (Prov. 25:2). God wants to inspire in us a holy desperation to encounter His beauty, that we should refuse to be comforted until we take hold of Him as our greatest treasure.

CHAPTER 7

"Kiss the Son Lest He Be Angry"

Most of us would want to know what lies in store for the church. What is going on behind the chaos in the world today?

Psalm 2 gives us insight into what lies behind some of the international conflicts that we read about in the headlines of today's newspapers. This is a very well-known messianic psalm that gives us a prophetic description of End-Time conflict between the nations and God. It has had a partial fulfillment in history, yet know that its greatest fulfillment still lies in the future. It reveals the rebellion of the primary international leaders against God and His Word. This rebellion will culminate at the end of the age. It is ultimately a war between God and Satan to establish who will rule the passions of the human heart.

A DIVINE DRAMA

Charles Haddon Spurgeon, the famous nineteenth-century British preacher, described Psalm 2 in terms of a great four-act drama.[1] The curtain goes up, and in the action of the first three verses the rebellious kings and rulers of the earth act out their parts in history. Then the curtain closes. The second act opens with God the Father at center stage responding to the evil leaders. The curtain closes and opens again for the third act. This time Jesus has the starring role. King David takes the stage in the fourth act and sounds a warning that echoes down the corridors of time—reaching from David's day to the Second Coming of the Lord.

The plot of the drama centers around the unified rebellion of the kings and rulers of the earth against God's sovereign decree that He will give all the nations and ends of the earth to His Son as His inheritance.

Shhhh! It's time to take our seats. The play is about to begin.

Act one: Satan's agenda

As the curtain rises, the nations are in an uproar, and the rebellious kings and rulers of the earth are taking counsel together, plotting their strategy:

> Why do the nations rage,
> And the people plot a vain thing?
> The kings of the earth set themselves,
> And the rulers take counsel together,
> Against the LORD and against His Anointed, saying,
> "Let us break Their bonds in pieces
> And cast away Their cords from us."
>
> —PSALM 2:1–3, NKJV

The kings of the earth are challenging God's right to command their obedience and to give Jesus the affections of the human race as His possession (v. 8). Nothing in all creation is more significant to God than the soul of a human being. It is the seat of affection, where love and true worship flow. Who ultimately possesses the people's affections is of highest concern to the Father. We were made in His own image, uniquely designed for His holy purposes. God would only send His beloved Son to die for priceless, eternal human souls.

God designed the human soul to be passionate and committed. This is the only way that we can function to our fullest. Without abandonment to God, our heart sinks into restlessness, boredom, and frustration. We must have something in our lives that is worth giving everything up for. If we have nothing to die for, then we have nothing to live for. God intended our souls to be fascinated with Jesus. Our highest development and greatest fulfillment lie in worshiping and serving Jesus with all our heart.

As an inheritance, God the Father has promised His Son a church filled with people ablaze with affection. The Father would not insult His beloved Son by giving Him a bride that is bored, passive, and compromising.

Passionless Christianity is no threat to the devil. It is focused on activities to the neglect of heartfelt affection and obedience to God. True Christianity sparks a flame in the human spirit. It ignites the heart with fervency.

Satan, aware of the Father's agenda to fill the church with passion for His Son, has an agenda of his own. To carry out his plans, Satan is raising up wicked leaders who are committed to sin. These leaders will violently oppose the idea of a passionate people filled with affection for Jesus. They are passionate in their resistance against the holy things of God. This passion will become a hellish rage against Jesus just before He returns. This raging conflict will be fought on many different battlegrounds: religious, social, and political ideologies; the economy; science and medicine; morals and ethics; education, music, and art.

Satan's underlying motive goes far beyond a particular issue in society. His desire is to win the passions of the human race that rightfully belong to Jesus. His goal is for the nations to erupt in rage against God. He is after a militant, unified, passionate revolt against God's laws and Jesus' right to reign over the planet.

If you keep an eye on the spiritual temperature of national and international events, you will see the thermometer climbing higher and higher. Look at the nations in the Western world. Pockets of anger and rebellion are smoldering among those who influence and set the course of morality. Satan and his cohorts are fanning flames to explode in rage and reckless revolt against God's ways.

First, he deceives the leaders. Then he unites them around his diabolical purposes. He motivates them to devise clever ploys to capture public opinion and undermine righteousness. He provokes them to cast off the restraints of God's written Word. They plot to erase the wise boundaries of right and wrong, good and evil that God has marked out in His Word for benefit of the human soul.

These deceived rulers boldly challenge the Father's right to give Jesus His inheritance. "The kingdoms of this world belong to us!" they rage. "We will not give Jesus our obedience and affection. The passions of mankind belong to the kings and leaders of the earth! We—not Your Son—have the right to the affections of men!"

The momentum of unholy passion is building. Dark-minded rulers from every level of society—lawmakers, educators, corporate heads, entertainers, advertisers, religious leaders, media moguls, and others plot to attack the holy commandments of God. They seek first to dilute, then to demolish them from society, one by one.

"We will not obey You!" they sneer. "We will break Your Word in pieces and cast away Your commandments. Right and wrong are only what we decide. We will do as we please. We live for our pleasure and not Yours. We will not worship You; we worship mankind!"

As the angry shouts and jeers of the wicked grow louder, the curtain falls on act one.

Act two: God's agenda

As act two opens, the Father is seated upon His throne, mocking the rebellious kings of the earth and laughing at their vain schemes and foolish plots to overthrown His purposes:

> He who sits in the heavens shall laugh;
> The LORD shall hold them in derision.
> Then He shall speak to them in His wrath,
> And distress them in His deep displeasure:
> "Yet have I set My King
> On My holy hill of Zion."
>
> —PSALM 2:4–6, NKJV

God's scoffing and mocking laughter at the foolish plot of these wicked kings is terrifying. The kings of the earth think they own the money of the earth. They think they hold the power and can make their own laws without any consequences from God. In their view, they ultimately control the world's systems and institutions. Science and technology have become tools to serve their wicked purposes. The rebellious rulers think that if they work together in unity, they can overrule God's purposes for Planet Earth.

God laughs at them, because He knows that their success is only because He Himself has granted it to them. The nations are as a drop in a bucket to Him (Isa. 40:15). The nations have no ability to permanently overthrow God's plans. The Father can bring an end to them with the mere flick of His finger. He can blow them away with the faintest breath from His mouth. He will release His End-Time judgments as described in the Book of Revelation to utterly destroy the kingdoms of this world that resist Him (Rev. 11:15–18).

"I have news for you," the Father might say. "I have *already* appointed My King on His holy hill. The inheritance of My Son is sure and forever. People of all ages, races, languages, and nations will be filled with holy passion for My Son. He will have a passionate church."

Revealing what is soon to come, act two closes as the battle lines are drawn. The people of the earth, now radically abandoned to one of two clear-cut agendas, take their places on one side or the other.

Act three: the Son claims His inheritance

Standing in center stage as the curtain rises is the anointed One, Jesus Christ. Jesus proclaims boldly:

> I will declare [the Father's] decree:
> The LORD has said to Me,
> "You are My Son,
> Today I have begotten You.
> Ask of Me, and I will give You
> The nations for Your inheritance,
> And the ends of the earth for Your possession.
> You shall break them with a rod of iron;
> You shall dash them to pieces like a potter's vessel."
>
> —PSALM 2:7–9, NKJV

The Father has already decreed His plans and provision to establish Jesus as King over all nations. Zechariah prophesied that Jesus would be king over all the earth (Zech. 14:9). Scripture describes an inheritance for the church as well as one for His Son.

We have an inheritance in Christ. But the Father has ordained that Christ has an inheritance in us (Eph. 1:17–18). Our inheritance includes receiving Jesus' love as His bride and His authority as coheirs and sons of God (Rom. 8:15–17). Jesus' inheritance in us includes our being fully possessed by Him. He will possess the nations as a people who fully love and obey Him. The Father called Jesus to intercede for the release of His inheritance on earth:

Ask of Me, and I will give You

The nations for Your inheritance,

And the ends of the earth for Your possession.

—PSALM 2:8, NKJV

In the final hours before His crucifixion, Jesus engaged in that intercession, praying for all believers. (See John 17:20–26.) At this very moment He is still interceding in heaven for His people who are His eternal inheritance (Heb. 7:25.)

Jesus seeks to rule with kindness, for it is the kindness of God that leads us to repentance (Rom. 2:4). However, if kindness is refused, then Jesus will use His terrifying judgments. His iron scepter will dash the rebellious nations to pieces, shattering them effortlessly like pottery.

What riches God has offered mankind. What dignity and destiny He has bestowed upon the human race by allowing us to be His people. We can only receive this as we voluntarily yield ourselves to the lordship of Jesus. Yet so few actually say yes to this.

The most powerful witness we can give unbelievers is a radiant life that shows forth that the will of God is good, acceptable, and perfect (Rom. 12:1–2). Unbelievers are looking for a church that is joyfully abandoned to Jesus' lordship. The unbelieving world mostly sees the church as spiritually bored and compromising with darkness. They will respond differently when they see a passionate church. Jesus is worthy of our total commitment. When we show forth this reality by our lives, then the multitudes in the nations will be saved (Rev. 7:9). I am very confident that they will see God's people taking up their crosses and turning their backs to sin as they love God with all their heart and strength (Deut. 30:6).

Act four: David's solemn warning

The curtain rises, and King David steps forward to enact the last scene of the drama. He issues a solemn threefold warning to all who are foolish enough to believe they can challenge God and prevail:

> Now therefore, be wise, O kings;
> Be instructed, you judges of the earth.
> Serve the LORD with fear,
> And rejoice with trembling.
> Kiss the Son, lest He be angry,
> And you perish in the way,
> When His wrath is kindled but a little.
> Blessed are all those who put their trust in Him.
>
> —PSALM 2:10–12, NKJV

"Serve the LORD with fear, and rejoice with trembling. Kiss the Son, lest He be angry," warns David.

God is awesome in splendor and terrifying in His greatness. This royal One has no superior—no equal. When we get a glimpse of His eternal power and majestic beauty, we will be filled with reverential fear. We tremble before His greatness.

If we feel only trembling in God's presence, then we will not experience the fullness of His grace. David says we are to rejoice before Him as well. We are to exult in the benefits of our inheritance.

There is yet another dimension. "Kiss the Son," says David, speaking symbolically of our affections being filled with passion for Jesus (Matt. 22:37; John 17:26). There is an intimate dimension in our relationship with God that is central to God's eternal salvation purposes as His bride (Rev. 19:7–8).

Some churches emphasize awe and trembling. Historically, some Holiness-type churches have focused on God's greatness, yet often leaving little room for rejoicing and affectionate worship.

Others concentrate on rejoicing in God's blessing. They focus almost entirely on the authority of the believer and the benefits that we receive in Christ. This is a vital part of our salvation, but we must not neglect to tremble before His awesome majesty and judgments—nor overlook the glory of "kissing the Son." Still others are focused only on the intimacy-with-God message while neglecting to walk in their authority that releases God's blessings. God has fashioned the human spirit in such a way that we need all three dimensions—trembling, rejoicing, and kissing—in our relationship with Him.

How about you? Are you committed to one dimension but not to the other two? Are two of these dimensions developing in your relationship with Him, but not the third?

Maybe you have only seen a holy God who judges rebellion, and so you seek to walk in faithfulness as you fear God. You understand what it means to tremble. Do you rejoice in the benefits that are yours in Christ?

Perhaps you do not experience much intimacy with God. The thought of kissing Christ makes you uncomfortable. It should, because David's call to kiss the Son is symbolic language that was not meant to be interpreted as literal kissing. It refers to receiving God's love and then responding back to Him with wholehearted love. The Holy Spirit pours love into our hearts (Rom. 5:5) and thus equips us to walk in this exchange of heart-ravishing love with God.

When I first read Psalm 2:12, I was troubled because I did not realize it spoke symbolically of heart adoration. As God dealt tenderly with me in my repeated failures, I began to understand His kindness and love. Thus, my heart began to overflow with adoration for God. I felt such gratitude and confidence in His presence.

In this, we respond with love to God because of the great love that He shows us. Truly, we love Him because we understand that He first loved us (1 John 4:19).

The Lord wants to intertwine these three dimensions in you. He wants to bring them forth by His Holy Spirit. This threefold response of trembling, rejoicing, and kissing is what comprises the inheritance promised to Jesus by the Father.

Finally, King David issues a warning to all who would be foolish enough to defy God: "Kiss the Son, lest He be angry, and you perish in the way, when His wrath is kindled but a little" (Ps. 2:12, NKJV). The lines of battle are being drawn even now in the nations. Who will control the affections of the human race? The Captain of the armies of heaven is Jesus. He has never lost a battle. He shall have His inheritance.

CHAPTER 8

STRONGHOLDS OF THE MIND

I was twenty-three years old and pastoring a church in St. Louis in 1978 when Luke, my first son, was born. The day after Luke's birth I had appointments I simply could not cancel. By the time the last appointment rolled around, I was aching so badly to see my one-day-old son that I couldn't even listen to the person talking to me.

Finally I broke away, jumped into my car, and went speeding down the road to see that little guy named Luke. I had this incredible ache, this urgent longing to be with my new son, to look into his face.

Suddenly an overwhelming realization hit my heart, and I found myself asking, "You mean, God, that the way I feel about my little Lukey is the way You feel about me?"

A question came to my mind: "How much do you love your son?"

"Oh, Lord," I said aloud, "I would give everything to this boy—everything!"

Then this scripture exploded in my heart:

If you then, being evil, know how to give good gifts to your children, how much more shall your Father who is in heaven give what is good to those who ask Him!

—MATTHEW 7:11

The realization of the magnitude of the Father's love for me—that God loved me much more than I loved my new son—was emotionally overpowering. I pulled to the side of the road and wept in my new understanding of the Father's love.

Many of the problems in the body of Christ today are the result of a more fundamental problem at the heart of the church. Our generation is paying a heavy price for the decline of the knowledge of God's heart. It is evident as we count the number of spiritual leaders who have fallen in their morality as well as the increase in financial scandals in the church. This woeful decline has brought about the secularizing of our churches and the decay of our inner lives, resulting in spiritual boredom and compromise. A. W. Tozer placed his finger squarely on the problem when he wrote:

> A condition…has existed in the church for some years and is steadily growing worse. I refer to the loss of the concept of majesty from the popular religious mind. The church has surrendered her once lofty concept of God and has substituted for it one so low, so ignoble, as to be utterly unworthy of thinking, worshiping men. This she has done not deliberately, but little by little and without her knowledge; and her very unawareness only makes her situation all the more tragic. The low view of God entertained almost universally among Christians is the cause of a hundred lesser evils everywhere among us.[1]

Christianity in America and much of the world is not God-centered. It's centered on needs, success, wholeness, or spiritual gifts. Although all these issues are important, they are not to be our primary focus, but rather a by-product of genuine spirituality. Emotional, spiritual, and physical blessings are a sure overflow from God-centered Christianity.

The church, having neglected her diligent pursuit of the knowledge of God, sometimes referred to as intimacy with God, has lost her joy and affection and the consciousness of His divine presence. She has lost her spirit of worship and her sense of awe and adoration. She has replaced encountering God with ministry success and substituted religious activity for heartfelt relationship with God.

A GOD IN OUR IMAGE

We have taken God for granted. We have allowed materialism, secularism, and the love of things to smother the flame of God in our souls. We have created God in our own image, an image that is erroneous and tragically inadequate. Many in our generation have made for themselves a God they can use and control—a "heavenly butler" who waits on them hand and foot, catering to their every whim. Others have fashioned a jovial, one-of-the-guys kind of God who understands mankind's necessity to lie or cheat or indulge in a harmless little sexual diversion now and then.

To some believers, God is warm, approachable, and forgiving. To others, He is cold, aloof, and condemning. Regardless of how we see Him, what you and I think about God is the most important thing about us. We will eventually be shaped by the image of God we carry in our minds.

Individuals often come to me with inaccurate, inadequate concepts of God's love and forgiveness. I may explain over and over, "God loves you, and He has forgiven you," but the believer responds, "I don't feel as if He loves me. I feel as if God has a big hammer in His hand, and He's just waiting to find a good enough reason to hit me over the head."

I may counsel and pray with the person time and time again, ministering the love and forgiveness of God, only to hear the individual say, "I wish I could believe that God is the way you say He is. I want to believe He really loves me, but I just can't grasp it."

Do you see how that person's life is being shaped by his or her inadequate concepts of God? As long as the individual continues to believe these or other lies about God and His nature, he or she will never mature into a strong Christian. That person will live in fear, insecurity, and defeat. Sooner or later, those fears and insecurities will bear poisonous fruit in the individual's own life and relationships with others.

I know it did in my own life. In the early years of my ministry I felt too guilty to minister to others if I was going through a period of personal failure or temptation. I did not want to pray for people—I did not think my prayers would help them.

I compared my experience to the days when I played college football. If I had had several bad days of practice, the coach would not let me play in the game that week. I thought God was like that: either I did great in practice, in my personal spiritual life, or I was disqualified from participating in ministry.

Today I am often amazed at how God uses me in ministry at those times when I feel most inadequate spiritually. But I have learned that God's strength is still present in my weakness.

Satan goes to great lengths to distort our concepts of God. But because such distortions can serve his "interests" in our lives, Satan is willing to invest as much time and work as it takes to secure those vulnerable areas of our minds for his own purposes.

We dare not decide to ignore and just learn to live with the lies and misconceptions about God's personality that have been planted there. Those inaccurate, inadequate concepts place us in great peril. To the degree that our ideas about God are lower than the truth of God, to that degree we are surely weakened and defeated. In those places and upon the foundation of distorted truth Satan is able to gain ground and set up his strongholds in our lives.

STRONGHOLDS OF THE MIND

For the weapons of our warfare are not of the flesh, but divinely powerful for the destruction of fortresses. We are destroying speculations and every lofty thing raised up against the knowledge of God, and we are taking every thought captive to the obedience of Christ.

—2 CORINTHIANS 10:4–5

What exactly does Paul mean by a stronghold? In ancient times, many strongholds were fortresses built with thick stone walls to protect a city from an evading enemy. Paul compared our warfare with Satan to a familiar idea in the ancient world, that of *stronghold*. A spiritual stronghold in the mind is made of a collection of wrong thoughts that disagree with God and agree with Satan.

Just as natural strongholds in the ancient world were made up of stones, so spiritual strongholds in our minds are made up of thoughts that accuse the truth about God and who we are in Christ. Paul used the idea of a spiritual stronghold or fortress to describe wrong thinking that exalts itself against the knowledge of God, thus giving the enemy a "protected place" of influence in our thought life. Wrong thoughts provide a "fortified" dwelling place of demonic influence in our minds and hearts.

Wrong ideas about God are not automatically eliminated when we are born again. Paul instructs the believers in Colossae to "put on the new self who is *being renewed* to a true knowledge according to the image" of God (Col. 3:10, emphasis added). We are continually in the process of being renewed by a truth about the personality of God.

EXPOSING SATAN'S STRONGHOLDS

Jesus made a statement about Himself with regard to Satan: "The ruler of the world…has nothing in Me" (John 14:30).

Jesus had no sin, wrong thinking, or impure motives that gave Satan legal access to His life. Satan could find *nothing* in Jesus—not even one inch of territory—to which he could lay claim and thus gain access to Jesus' heart.

The enemy continually seeks occasions where he can obtain a legal entry point into our lives. Sin and spiritual ignorance open the door and invite his hold over us. As a shark is drawn to blood, so the devil is drawn to lies and darkness. When I speak of areas of spiritual darkness, I'm not referring to a random sinful action here and there, but to an area where truth has been usurped by a lie inside our minds.

Paul explained this darkness as being like a veil that obscures the liberating light of the gospel in the minds of unbelievers:

> …that they might not see the light of the gospel of the glory of Christ, who is the image of God.
>
> —2 Corinthians 4:4

Here Paul tells us what the light is. The light is the understanding of the gospel of the glory of Christ. In other words, understanding the glory of Christ includes understanding who He is in His personality and what He did in His redemptive work on the cross for us.

> For God, who said, "Light shall shine out of darkness," is the One who has shone in our hearts to give the light of the knowledge of the glory of God in the face of Christ.
>
> —2 Corinthians 4:6

What is the light of the gospel? It is the knowledge of the glory of God as manifested in Jesus' personality and His work on the cross.

Satan's goal is to keep us in darkness. His strategy is to distort our knowledge of God so that it is erroneous and inadequate. Thus we are weakened and held in bondage. Satan does not want the light of the knowledge of God's heart to invade our spiritual darkness. He seeks to lay claim to every area of spiritual darkness that he can find in us, including wrong ideas and thought systems, sympathetic thoughts toward sin, and self-excusing rationalizations. He utilizes these to erect spiritual *strongholds* in us that protect his investments and interests in our lives.

LEARNING MORE ABOUT STRONGHOLDS

As a young Christian I had a certain zeal to discipline myself to gain spiritual ground so that I could earn God's affection and favor. When I succeeded, I became spiritually proud. When I failed, I felt condemned. Eventually I recognized that, like the Pharisees of old, I was trying to earn God's favor by my spiritual disciplines and achievements.

How does the enemy construct a spiritual stronghold in our lives? First, he starts with a foundation of lies and half-truths. Usually these are lies about the personality of God or about how God views us. Next, up go thick spiritual walls, brick by brick. They are built by inaccurate ideas about God and distorted perceptions of how God sees and feels about us, especially in our spiritual immaturity and when we sin. Held together by the mortar of mistaken reasoning, the walls rise higher and higher. Soon lofty spiritual towers of vain imaginations loom inside us. Satan erects every stronghold he can to keep us from the true knowledge of God. To the degree he is successful, we will not enjoy an intimate relationship with the Lord.

We must adopt an offensive posture if we are to break free from a spiritual stronghold. If we are to be free, then we must know the truth about the personality of God and how He views us in Christ.

In John 8:32 Jesus said, "You shall know the truth, and the truth shall make you free."

We must know truth. Our fierce determination to overcome our sinful weaknesses is not enough. We must fuel our mind with truth.

UNDERSTANDING GOD'S LOVE FOR US

Most Christians have vague or inaccurate ideas about God's personality. Our ideas often come from our relationships with earthly authority figures. As we think of the authority figures who were the most influential in our early years, we will discover that many of our ideas about God are connected to how we perceived these people.

Often the most significant person in the forming of these ideas is the person's earthly father. Also important are mothers or perhaps an athletic coach, a schoolteacher, a tutor, or even a piano teacher—anyone who is looked up to and admired.

Our experience with these authority figures affected us emotionally in our early years. The following descriptions of different types of father figures give us insight into how some of us have formed our ideas of God.

The passive father

The passive father is emotionally distant; that is, he expresses his affections in a very minimal way. He assumes that you know that he loves you. He rarely speaks it to you. He rarely expresses his feelings in an open way, whether pain or joy. When something wonderful or tragic happens, the passive father usually just nods his head.

Some people who have grown up with this type of father think that their heavenly Father is like their earthly passive father. In other words, they think that God does not feel their pain or share their joy, or that He has little or no affection to express toward them. Those who grew up with this type of father usually have difficulty believing that God is interested in their lives. They assume that God does not really care about what is in their hearts or the pressures that they are withstanding.

The authoritarian father

The authoritarian father intervenes in a strong way to stop what you are doing. He hands out a clear list of dos and don'ts. He interrupts you when you talk and minimizes the things that are important to you. Thus, as you grow up, your heart is quenched by this style of communication.

This type of father does not honor the individuality of his children. He is not deeply interested in what their desires or goals are—only his own. He does not desire real partnership or intimacy with his children. His primary concern is to be obeyed, not to develop a relationship. Those who grew up with this type of father usually have difficulty understanding that God wants more than service and sacrifice. They assume that God is not interested in having a real relationship with them. They view the kingdom of God as a series of sacrifices for the "great cause," without a paradigm that God longs for intimate partnership with His children.

The abusive father

Abusive fathers inflict pain on their children deliberately, hurting them emotionally, mentally, physically, and sometimes sexually. There is no greater torment in life than the torment at the hands of an abusive father. Not only does it damage a child's thinking and emotional process, thus greatly influencing their behavior throughout their life, but it also ruins how the child relates to God.

Those who grew up with this type of father draw back from abandoning themselves to God. They fear that God will treat them harshly simply because He has the power to do anything He likes. They assume God's will is always harsh and difficult. This mind-set can easily receive the great lie that they have given up more for God than what God has given them in return.

The absent father

The fourth type of father is one who is totally absent. He may be the father you never knew because of death, divorce, or abandonment, or maybe he lived at home but you rarely saw him because he was a workaholic. He is not like the passive father who is there yet does not communicate. He simply is not there. Therefore he does not intervene to help the child in times of confusion or trouble. The child often has strong feelings of abandonment because of his father.

Those who grew up with this type of father usually have difficulty receiving affirmation and affection from their heavenly Father. They assume that God has also abandoned them when they need Him most.

The accusing father

The fifth father-figure type is the most common example. He is the accusing father. He proclaims to love you with his whole heart, but he judges you continually at every failure. In his mind he is trying to motivate you to do right. He thinks that if he points out your failures, you will be motivated to try harder next time. He rarely shows you affection or affirms you. If you grew up with this type of father, you will have great difficulty understanding the love of your heavenly Father because you will think God is always accusing you.

God is not like any earthly authority figures. In Psalm 50:21 we read that God said, "You thought that I was altogether like you" (NKJV). Through Isaiah the Lord said, "My thoughts are not your thoughts, nor are your ways My ways....For as the heavens are higher than the earth, so are My ways higher than your ways" (Isa. 55:8–9, NKJV).

As high as the heavens are above the earth, so God's affections and tender mercy are higher than man's. In other words, the greatest father on the earth falls infinitely short of the love and tender concern that our heavenly Father has for us. There is no human model that gives an adequate picture of the passions of God's heart for us.

Some people only know a father who constantly ridiculed them. Some know a father who molested them. Others were beaten physically. Some had a father that was a drug addict, an alcoholic, or was in prison. Often, these images of an authority figure transfer to their view of God's personality.

As the Scriptures and the Holy Spirit introduce us to a smiling God, it changes our entire life. I can remember when I began to think of a God with a big smile on His face when He thought of me. I imagined Him saying, "I enjoy you—knowing you brings pleasure to My heart."

I initially struggled with thoughts that are all too common to many of us: "Who, me? Did You see my sin? How can You enjoy me when I have such weaknesses?" However, the Father would answer through the counsel of His Word, "I see the sincerity in your heart. I see the cry in your heart to please Me even though you often stumble. I delight in My relationship with you!"

As I recognized this glad God with a smile on His face, I realized that I had an entirely wrong idea of what His personality was like. I saw that He wanted me to run *to* Him, not *away* from Him when I failed.

I've been in the ministry for thirty years. Through those years I have grieved with many who have told me stories of their terrible hardships—stories of molestation, abuse, and perversion at the hands of cruel and hateful people. But I know that even if they had never experienced real love, God's Word offers each one bondage-breaking truth and joyful hope through the revelation of God's heart for them.

The knowledge of God's pure, faithful, passionate affection for us is more powerful and life transforming than anything we can receive from our earthly father. It is the Holy Spirit, not human witnesses, who reveals God's love for us and makes Him real to our hearts, *and that revelation is available to everyone.*

People with wounded and broken spirits, or perfectionists with performance-driven personalities, often have difficulty receiving from God. Sometimes we become so caught up in our own pressures, pain, or anger that we don't even recognize His voice. As we persist in receiving the truth of God's Word about God's heart for us, then our hearts can progressively be healed of what earthly authority figures have done to us. The Holy Spirit will reveal the Word of God to us, giving us new and fresh understanding about the passionate affection in God's heart for us.

Neither good experiences from our fathers nor even our zeal for God can produce abounding love for Jesus in us. I was an angry, frustrated Christian who constantly carried a heavy burden of guilt and failure for not measuring up. Only when I began to see the true knowledge of how God feels about me did the spiritual strongholds in my mind and heart begin to break down. One passage that greatly strengthened me said:

> Love has been perfected among us in this: that we may have boldness in the day of judgment; because as He is, so are we in this world. There is no fear in love; but perfect love casts out fear, because fear involves torment. But he who fears has not been made perfect in love.
>
> —1 JOHN 4:17–18, NKJV

The person who is afraid of God, who fears that He will judge all their failings, will live in torment. Torment is the opposite of boldness. When I recognized that God's heart is filled with tenderness for me—even in my weakness—then it made me bold in my love for God.

God, who has never painted the same sunset twice, knows exactly how to reveal Himself to you. He will choose the perfect time and way to speak to you. He knows the precise way to illuminate your understanding, feed your hungry heart, or flow like healing oil over your wounded spirit. When you come to your heavenly Father for help, you will not be ignored or rebuked. You will not be ridiculed for your mistakes. He is extraordinarily kind and very patient toward you. He cares for you with affection and watchfulness. His love for you will never fail or end.

It's wonderful to have known people who showed us what God is really like. Their examples can help prepare the way for God's work in our lives or even speed up the process. But if we have never known even one loving, godly person, we can still experience personal wholeness and be filled with passionate affection for Jesus. God, His Word, and the Holy Spirit's work in our lives are sufficient to bring us to personal wholeness and spiritual maturity.

RECOVERING THE TRUE KNOWLEDGE OF GOD

What will cure the "hundred lesser evils that are everywhere among us"?[2] Only the knowledge of God's personality. Knowing how He views us in Christ will strengthen the inner man and demolish Satan's strongholds.

Christianity must again become God-centered. I agree with Tozer; as we recover that lofty concept of God and rediscover His majesty and His tender mercy, the church will be dynamically transformed. We must practice long and loving meditation on the truths of the Scriptures and the being of God. Only one thing will ever satisfy our deep cravings. We must come to know God as He is: the excellencies of His person, His extravagant emotions, and His ravished heart (Song of Sol. 4:9). The church knows Jesus as her Savior. But the Son of God is getting ready to reveal Himself as her Beloved, clothed in majesty and beauty (Isa. 33:17). His love will ignite the passions of His people. A spiritually bored church is about to be swept off her feet!

CHAPTER 9

Igniting Holy Passion

A faithful Christian woman in her early forties gathered the courage after many years to resign from her job, leave the home of her godly parents, and go to work for a missions organization overseas. Molested as a child, she had lived much of her life controlled by fear. She had not yet overcome these fears, but her sparkling eyes and bubbly personality covered up her lack of confidence and low self-esteem. She longed to marry a godly Christian and serve the Lord with him, but the right man had never come along. The woman was therefore surprised and pleased when a single Christian man about her age who worked for the same missions group began showing her attention—warm smiles, genuine appreciation for her conscientious work, little compliments dropped here and there. She was even more surprised when he suggested that they begin having lunch together several times a week.

She felt so plain. So ordinary. So undesirable. But the more the woman got to know her new friend, the more she liked and respected him. She could tell the feelings were mutual.

One day at work the man asked if he could take her out for dinner. That evening she glanced up from the menu and saw him gazing at her with a tender, loving expression in his eyes. "I'm sorry for staring," he said, a little embarrassed, "but you are so beautiful that you take my breath away."

The woman could hardly believe her ears. *Beautiful! Me?* She opened her mouth to protest and put herself down, but something stopped her. *He sees you the way I see you,* an inner thought seemed to say. Overwhelmed beyond words, the woman's face broke into a radiant smile.

How do you think God sees you? Do you cringe at the thought? God's estimation of your beauty comes from His great love for you—not as a result of any inherent goodness or beauty of your own.

God is not the cold, aloof, rigidly legalistic being that religion has made Him out to be. He is not the demanding, impatient God so many of us have struggled to please. Oh, how the Lord longs for His church to receive a revelation of His ravished heart—filled with delight for us—even though we may not like or believe in ourselves. How His heart aches for us to become aware of His desire for us (Ps. 45:11).

Our God is not a thing or an it. He is an affectionate, loving, deeply passionate being. Today's church desperately needs a renewed understanding of the nature of God's personality and a new comprehension of His passion for us.

THE MISSING DIMENSION OF OUR REDEMPTION

The Reformers and their successors saw many changes in the way the church understood salvation by rediscovering the essential truth of the gospel—that we are justified by faith alone (Rom. 3:21–31). What a liberating experience it was for people to understand that the gift of righteousness could be received simply by faith. It was like coming out of darkness into the daylight. Salvation involves a glorious exchange in which Christ takes our sin and guilt, and we take on His righteousness as a totally free gift. I love the doctrine of salvation that highlights our legal position in Christ. I believe it is a vital dimension to the preaching of the cross and is foundational to a healthy walk with God.

In some places even the glories of reformed evangelicalism have become rigid and scholastic. The whole of one's relationship with God is often defined in terms of legal standing with Him. God is the judge who stamps *accepted* on our heavenly passport, then turns and says, "Next!" That's good news, but that is not all the good news. In a relationship defined by law, a believer is not aware of a God whose heart is ravished—enraptured and filled with delight—for His people.

Salvation is more than a legal exchange affecting our position before God. Salvation also includes the exchange of deep affections and love. As God communicates His enjoyment and affections for us, we in turn respond in a similar way. John said it best: "We love Him because He first loved us" (1 John 4:19, NKJV). An intellectual understanding of the legal aspects of salvation is essential, but it is not the full counsel of God.

We will never have more passion for God than we understand that He has for us. We will never be more committed to God than our understanding of His commitment to us.

The Holy Spirit must quicken our knowledge of God's passionate love as the way He has chosen to impart it in our hearts—a God whose personality overflows with deep emotions for His people. The proclamation of the passionate heart of God must pulsate at the core of our ministry, whether in our teaching on how to be saved, how to minister to the sick, or in how to lead a home group.

Although God is totally self-sufficient, He desires our love. He who has no need of us has bound His heart to us forever. He did this freely because He delights in loving us:

> In this is love, not that we loved God, but that He loved us and sent His Son to be the propitiation for our sins.
>
> —1 John 4:10, NKJV

...having predestined us to adoption as sons...according to the good pleasure of His will.

—EPHESIANS 1:5, NKJV

The affectionate heart of God swelled with pleasure as He established our salvation that leads to being adopted as His children. It is much easier to receive that God loves us when we walk in mature obedience. But God enjoys us long before we mature. Even when we are coming up short, He sees our hearts toward Him.

The Book of Romans contains the *legal, earthly, practical dimension* of our redemption. The Book of Revelation reveals the *eternal, majestic dimension* of our redemption. The Song of Solomon extols the *passionate, affectionate dimension* of our redemption. All three of these dimensions will come together in a thorough understanding of our relationship to God as mentioned in Psalm 2:

Serve the LORD with fear,
And rejoice with trembling.
Kiss the Son, lest He be angry,
And you perish in the way.

—PSALM 2:11–12, NKJV

We rejoice in the free gift of salvation as seen in Romans, we tremble at His majesty as seen in Revelation, and we kiss the Son in response to His affection as revealed in the Song of Solomon.

The Song of Solomon can be accurately interpreted in at least two different ways. Historically, it depicts King Solomon's wooing and wedding of a young shepherdess, and it describes the beauty of married love between a man and his wife. Allegorically, it speaks of the love King Jesus has for His bride, the church. The Holy Spirit will apply this book to the church in both ways.

For three chapters, I will concentrate on the application that shows King Jesus' love song to His bride. This view of the Song of Solomon needs to be taught often. It will wash the church as it prophetically calls her forth to holy passion.

THE PROGRESSION OF HOLY PASSION

In this love song from heaven, the Shulamite maiden is the maturing church, as the bride of Christ. I see a clear spiritual progression in the eight chapters of the Song of Solomon. It is a divine pattern revealing the progression of holy passion in the heart of the church as the beauty and affection of her glorious King woo her.

I want to focus on two benefits from meditating upon this great prophetic song of redemptive love. First, the Holy Spirit unveils to us the passions and pleasures in the personality of the Son of God. This gives us insight into the heart of Jesus, which in turn energizes us with new passion for Him. Second, as we meditate upon the Song of Solomon, we may identify our experience in this divine pattern as we continue on our journey toward Christian maturity. As we understand more of the stages that God will take us through on our journey to fullness, then we are comforted and renewed. This brings increased ability to cooperate courageously and confidently with the Spirit's work in us during each stage of our journey with Him.

The awakening to fervency—Song of Solomon 1:2

There comes a time in the lives of mature believers when we are first awakened to holy fervency for God. When we cry, "God, I'm tired of serving You from a distance. I do not care what it will cost. I want to be totally Yours in the deepest part of my being."

I will never forget the feeling that flooded my being when I realized that the great invisible God who created the earth and everything in it actually listened to me when I talked to Him. He actually responded to my requests.

I clearly remember how God touched me when I was only nineteen years old and agreed to lead the youth group's annual ski trip. Five young people signed up for the trip who did not have the money to go. I told them they could come because the Lord would provide. That was a new idea to me at that time of my life. I had no money to pay their way. I asked the Lord for help. Someone who knew nothing of this financial need approached me on the day we were to leave and gave me a check for very amount that was needed. This provision impacted the way I had previously viewed God. It was life changing for me. He knew the need and dilemma, and it deeply warmed my heart toward Him. It has been years since then, but I will never forget the feeling I had on that day.

That simple experience sparked a flame of fervency in my spirit. The progression of passion starts with this fresh awakening to holy fervency. But fervency is not the same thing as maturity. It is only a beginning.

The Song of Solomon opens with the great cry for more of Jesus: "May he kiss me with the kisses of his mouth! For your love is better than wine" (Song of Sol. 1:2). This speaks figuratively of our cry for the "kiss of His Word" or for intimacy with God that comes through His Word. This is not the casual kiss on the cheek from a relative or friend. Spiritually it speaks of the cry of our spirit for deeper intimacy with Jesus.

Our hunger for intimacy with Jesus will never be satisfied with simple "churchianity."

The young Shulamite maiden cried to her king, "Your love is better than wine." In the same spirit, we as believers today are coming to the point where we realize money and material comforts will never answer the cry of our spirits. Prominence in ministry or the world will never do it. No sensual or romantic relationship with another human being will ever satisfy the deepest cravings of our spirits. We are becoming tired of powerless religion that cannot

deliver us from sin or from ourselves. We are tired of churches paralyzed in apathy.

A fresh abandonment, a new holy recklessness for Jesus, is
awakening in the spirits of God's people today. The Spirit of God
is calling us forth, taking the truths of time and eternity and using
them to awaken us out of complacency. Before Jesus returns, God
will raise up a church filled with people who are hungering for God-
centered Christianity and who refuse to return to man-centered
Christianity. The denominational label will not matter. If the Son
of God is being ministered in power, and if His beauty is being
unveiled, people will flock to Him.

Why do we want Him? We have discovered that the love and
affection of God are better than anything the world has to offer,
and we're beginning to see a little bit of the majesty and matchless
beauty of the love of Christ Jesus.

> Because of the fragrance of your good ointments,
> Your name is ointment poured forth.
> —Song of Solomon 1:3, nkjv

The lovely perfumed fragrance speaks symbolically of the
graces of Jesus' personality, the beauty of who He is, and the perfection of all He does. The irresistible aroma of His perfume will
capture the church again.

> We love Him because He first loved us.
> —1 John 4:19, nkjv

It takes God to love God. It takes a progressive revelation of
God's satisfying love, His exuberant affection, and His indescribable beauty to awaken the church and compel her to give herself
wholly back to Him. Like Paul, the church is best compelled to
wholeheartedness by this knowledge of God's love (2 Cor. 5:14).

Some look at people who have high-energy personalities and say, "If I were wired with 220 volts like them, I too would be filled with passion for God. But I have a different temperament. I'm one of those 110-volt folks; therefore, I do not have as much passion for God."

It is essential that we understand that passion for Jesus is not a natural personality trait. I assure you that people with a quiet personality can equally be filled with love for God as those with more outgoing personalities. They may not express their passion for God in the same way a "220-volt" type personality does, but that fiery love will equally be there, and it will be just as real and just as deep.

It takes the power of God to inspire and empower us to love God. The love of God is poured into the human spirit by the Holy Spirit (Rom. 5:5). It does not matter at all how much natural energy or zeal we possess in our personality. Passion for Jesus is the work of the Holy Spirit and is imparted to us as we recognize His passion for us. We will walk in commitment to Him only as we understand that He has a greater commitment to us.

Most of us have known some people who were spiritually hyped up for a year or two. But when the trials and tribulations came, all their frothy human zeal fizzled out and their love for Jesus cooled off. I recall my experience in my youth, when I ministered with a team of street preachers in campus ministry. Some of these zealous evangelists preached fiery sermons on the college campus. But within ten years many were not even walking with God. Their extraordinary zeal had led nowhere—except away from God. Their commitment to Jesus was short-lived because it was not anchored in the revelation of His commitment to them.

Beloved, Jesus is committed to and deeply loves those who are His. When we see the fragrances of the perfume of who He is and how He feels toward us, then we cry out, "Let me know the kisses of Your Word, our God."

Our immature fervency must be anchored in the revelation of the Lord's passion for us. Our immature love does indeed delight His heart. He knows that our fervency is not the same as spiritual maturity.

Prioritizing intimacy and ministry—Song of Solomon 1:4

After the maiden in the Song of Solomon awakens to fervency for Jesus, she then prays a twofold prayer: "Draw me after you and let us run together" (Song of Sol. 1:4). The order of that prayer is important. First we are drawn to Him in intimacy; then we run together with Him in ministry. If we are to become effective co-laborers with Christ, running with Him, we first must focus on being drawn as worshipers to encounter His affection for us.

It's easy for people to pray, "Let me run with You, Jesus," or "Increase my sphere of ministry and influence," without fervently seeking to be drawn near Him. God's order is that we be drawn to greater intimacy with Jesus as the way to greater effectiveness in ministry. That is what "running," or real ministry, is all about—bringing deliverance to the hearts of human beings so they can be drawn into knowing and worshiping God intimately.

On the other hand, a few believers say, "Draw me," but resist running with the Lord as a partner with Him in His work in the earth. The Holy Spirit does not draw us so we can hang up a "Do Not Disturb" sign and sit in our little comfort zone, only singing love songs to Jesus the rest of our lives. As fellow heirs with Christ, we are drawn into intimacy, and then empowered in ministry to bring others into intimacy with the Lord.

The church will surely mature in the tension of drawing and running. We will learn how to deliver broken people, prevail in spiritual warfare, and serve one another while maintaining our intimacy with Jesus. These two prayers, to be drawn and to run, correspond to the two great commandments Jesus gave in Matthew 22:37–40.

Being drawn into deep intimacy with Jesus fulfills the first commandment to love God with all our hearts, and running in servanthood ministry fulfills the second commandment to love our neighbors as ourselves.

Your life goal

In the first chapter of this beautiful love song we saw where the Shulamite maiden stated her intention (Song of Sol. 1:2–4). She laid out the goal and theme of her life on earth. She desired an intimate relationship with him whose love was better to her than the best wine of the world, and she desired to run in ministry so that she might impart this reality to others. From Song of Solomon 1:5 until the very end in Song of Solomon 8:14, we trace the maiden's spiritual journey in her progression of passion for her beloved king.

Whatever your vocation may be, you must align your life vision with this cry: to be drawn to Jesus in intimacy and then to run with Him in ministry to others. Whether you are a medical doctor, a schoolteacher, a preacher, a truck driver, a homeschooling mom— you must set your heart to know and worship God in an intimate way and be one who ministers God's grace to people.

It's important that you have goals. However, you must have one primary life goal that is bigger than all your other goals. If you do not know what your life goal is, ask the Lord to show you. Ask Him to draw you into intimacy with Him, then to empower you in ministry in any way that He desires. Is your spirit longing for a new awakening to the satisfying love of God? Do you want to know Him intimately?

O Lord, we have seen just a little bit of Your majesty. The beauty of who You are and what You do is capturing our hearts. From this point on I want my life to be one unbroken journey of progression in holy passion. Draw me, Lord. Draw me to Your glorious self. I don't want to be at a distance. I want You, no matter what it costs me. Draw me, Jesus, and I will run after You!

And as I run, I will learn to mature in obedience. But how?

CHAPTER 10

FERVENT—BUT IMMATURE

Spiritual fervency as it is portrayed by the Shulamite maiden in the last chapter is essential in our progression to spiritual maturity. However, as already stated, fervency is not the same as maturity. Our commitment to the Lord is usually much more superficial than we realize at first.

Like the maiden in the Song of Solomon, I have experienced difficulty in prioritizing intimacy and ministry. In my early life as a Christian I was more interested in ministering to Christians and witnessing to unbelievers than I was in spending quality time alone with God in devotional prayer. My heart grew cold because of this.

Even today, as the leader of the IHOP Missions Base, my life is still easily overwhelmed in context of a growing ministry. I find that my heart can be pulled away from retreating in private or distracted from developing my secret life with God.

Like the Shulamite maiden, all believers pass through a self-centered stage where our goals are primarily focused on receiving more blessings and experiencing more of Jesus' presence. Blessings and the thrill of spiritual experiences are perfectly legitimate, but they are not the final goal of mature Christianity.

LIVING IN THE PLEASURE OF HIS PRESENCE—
SONG OF SOLOMON 2:3–6

In the following verses, notice the maiden's emphasis on the spiritual pleasure she experiences. I imagine her exclaiming, "Just me and Jesus! This is all I want; this is all I need." As good as that initially sounds, God has more that He wants to work in us than receiving His blessings and enjoying His presence. The maiden proclaims:

"In his shade I took great delight and sat down,
And his fruit was sweet to my taste.
He has brought me to his banquet hall,
And his banner over me is love.
Sustain me with raisin cakes,
Refresh me with apples,
Because I am lovesick.
Let his left hand be under my head
And his right hand embrace me."

"I adjure you, O daughters of Jerusalem…
That you will not arouse or awaken my love
Until she pleases."
—Song of Solomon 2:3–7

Discovering that Jesus is the primary source of our spiritual delight is a very important part of our progression toward maturity. Notice that the Lord did not want this process disturbed in the maiden (v. 7). He has ordained specific spiritual seasons for our spiritual development. In fact, in this passage, the Holy Spirit asks the others to not stir her up or to not disturb her in this season of spiritual delight.

At this stage, we do not really understand the bigger picture. We have an inheritance in God, but God also has an inheritance in us. What an incredible thought: God, who possesses everything, has something He waits for—His inheritance in us (Eph. 1:11, 18).

In this stage, we are focused only on receiving our inheritance from God, not on being His inheritance. As far as we're concerned, Jesus is reigning in heaven solely for our pleasure and good. We know little about His passion to disciple the nations, little about faith that embraces risk and sacrifice, and little about the warfare that will be required on the journey. We will look at those subjects in the next chapter. Even so, while we are still in the process of discovering His beauty and delighting ourselves in Him, the Lord is bonding our hearts to Him. Because of this season, we will not be content with ministry that causes us to neglect our intimacy with Him.

Jesus may allow us to spend months or even years in this satisfying, secure, self-absorbed spiritual stage. Sometimes, by experiencing just a little of God's presence, we make the mistake of assuming we have found its zenith. But being saved and spiritually satisfied is only part of our inheritance and only a part of our spiritual journey. Our inheritance includes being equipped to be coheirs with Christ that experience the Father's heart, home, and throne forever (Rev. 3:21).

CHALLENGING THE COMFORT ZONE— SONG OF SOLOMON 2:8–17

Because the Lord loves us so deeply, He continues to give us new revelations of Himself. In this stage of this song of love, the Shulamite maiden sees her beloved king in an entirely different dimension. She watches as he comes to her, leaping and skipping on the mountaintops like a gazelle:

> The voice of my beloved!
> Behold, he comes
> Leaping upon the mountains,

Skipping upon the hills.

My beloved is like a gazelle....

He stands behind our wall;

He is looking through the windows....

My beloved spoke, and said to me:

"Rise up, my love, my fair one,

And come away."

—SONG OF SOLOMON 2:8–10, NKJV

The hills and mountains speak of obstacles that must be overcome as we walk with God. They include the trials and pressures that are a part of everyone's spiritual growth, and they refer to demonic principalities and powers. They may also include the kingdoms of this world that oppose the gospel. No obstacle is insurmountable for Jesus, who effortlessly leaps over them like a gazelle on a mountaintop. The Lord is revealing Himself to the maiden as the sovereign king of all nations who can effortlessly leap over the mountains. The maiden describes her beloved as standing outside her window calling her to arise and come away with him (v. 10).

In the early stages of our spiritual journeys, we may have seen Jesus as the One whose presence satisfies our heart, just as the maiden did. We must also see our Beloved as the sovereign king who effortlessly leaps over all obstacles as He manifests His authority over the nations.

As we seek to go on to maturity in our walk with Jesus, we will surely encounter Him as the mighty King who skips on mountains. In these seasons, He is challenging the comfort zone in our life as He calls us to join Him in His war against all that oppose His kingdom in this world. This includes being involved in spiritual warfare and in sacrificial service.

Can you recall a time when the Lord challenged you to arise and leave your comfort zone? He was in essence saying, "Arise, My beautiful one, and come with Me. You can't sit under the shade tree forever. Come and leap mountains with Me. Will you love Me enough to join Me in bringing My kingdom even to the places that oppose Me?"

She ended up refusing Jesus by telling Him, "Turn, my beloved, and be like a gazelle" (v. 17). In other words, she is telling Him to go leap on the mountains without her.

Just like this maiden, I have sometimes refused the Lord's fresh challenges by telling Him to go leap on the mountains or go and conquer areas of darkness without me. I admit that I've answered Him in this way before: "But Lord, I can't go. I don't want to leave my safe apple tree and my banquet table to conquer new territory of darkness with You." I would complain, "It took me years to get to the place where I really enjoyed just being with You. I don't want to lose it. I love You; I'm satisfied with just You and me."

In May 1999, the Lord challenged me to leave the comfort zone to join Him as He was calling me to a new venture in the kingdom with Him. I was pastoring the same church that I planted nearly eighteen years earlier. I was comfortable, and things were going well. The church had grown to about three thousand people, and our building was debt free. Things were going pretty good from a natural point of view. That is when the Lord said to me, "Come with Me." It was at that time that I began the International House of Prayer of Kansas City. This required that I resign from the church and give up my salary. For the first time in twenty-five years of ministry, I began to raise my own financial support. My wife agreed that it was God's will for us to make this move.

IHOP-KC started out in a small little building that we affectionately dubbed "the Bethlehem stable." I had a small band of young zealots with me. We had very few people and even less money. We were definitely out of our comfort zone. We did not know how to make this work, but we were trusting God as we followed Him.

A similar thing happened eighteen years earlier, before IHOP-KC, when the Lord called me to leave my young adult church in St. Louis, Missouri, to move to Kansas City, Missouri, and plant a new church. I was miserable as I wrestled with the Lord over this new challenge to leave my comfort zone. I didn't want to leave my dear friends in St. Louis. I greatly enjoyed pastoring that church. I wrestled with God every moment of every day. I couldn't pray or worship. There was such a clear sense of the withdrawing of His peace that, after two weeks, I could stand it no longer. In the middle of the night I finally got up and promised the Lord I would go. Peace finally came to my troubled heart.

The maiden refused to go with her beloved to the mountains because of fear, not rebellion. It was just human weakness. She was fervent—but immature.

Have you ever told the Lord no out of fear and weakness when He asked you to do something for Him? Just as He did with the maiden, the Lord calls us out of our comfort zone that we may become mature disciples who live for His pleasure and purpose. That is the theme of the remainder of the Song of Solomon.

EXPERIENCING THE LORD'S CORRECTION—
SONG OF SOLOMON 3:1–3

Our fear and weakness do not anger the Lord. That is all we really have to bring to Him. That's all He has to work with. But if we refuse to obey the Lord, He will discipline us because of His love for us. When we ask the Lord, as the maiden did in Song of Solomon 1:4, to draw us and let us run together with Him, that means leaving the security of the comfort zone and going to the mountains with Him when He calls us. Sometimes the Lord gets our attention in disciplining us by withdrawing His presence for a season. That is the way He caused the maiden to repent for refusing Him:

On my bed night after night I sought him
Whom my soul loves;
I sought him but did not find him.
"I must arise now and go about the city...
I must seek him whom my soul loves."
I sought him but did not find him.
The watchmen who make the rounds in the city found me,
And I said, "Have you seen him whom my soul loves?"
Scarcely had I left them
When I found him whom my soul loves;
I held on to him and would not let him go.
—Song of Solomon 3:1–4

When the Lord corrects His sincere, yet immature, disciples, He is not angry with us. He still loves and enjoys us in our immaturity; however, He loves us too much to let us stay there. Although we do not always understand it, He is bringing us forth to maturity. He knows what awaits us—the glory of being His bride and the spiritual treasures that come with being mature coheirs of the glorious Son of God.

With this in mind, He pries our fingers loose from the things to which we cling so tenaciously. Firmly, but tenderly, He woos us away from anything that would hold us back from that which is His best for our lives.

He could say to us, "If you only knew the glory that you will inherit, you would never refuse Me. Have I ever led you into a place where I could not meet you and provide for you? I will never take anything from you that will not be restored tenfold. My disciplines are good. They seem sorrowful for the moment, but afterward they yield the fruit of righteousness." (See Hebrews 12:5–13.)

After this time of gentle discipline, the maiden arises from her bed under the shade tree and searches throughout the entire city until she finds her beloved (Song of Sol. 3:2–4). When the Lord's presence departs from us in our place of compromise, just like this maiden, we must arise in obedience and faith and seek Him. I think I know what she said when she found her beloved. I've had to say it to the Lord a few times myself: "You win. I will obey. I must have Your presence, and I must know that I am pleasing to You. What is life without Your presence?"

AFFIRMING AND WOOING THE BRIDE— SONG OF SOLOMON 4:1–5

In this section of this great love song, the Lord proclaims to the maiden, "How beautiful you are, My love. How beautiful you are." Then He speaks eight specific prophetic affirmations over her life. Each affirmation is given in symbolic language that would have been easily understood in Solomon's day. In other words, the Lord is wooing the maiden as she decides to come forth in full obedience. Jesus often speaks over us as we timidly arise and take baby steps forward, purposing to leave the comfort zone and progress into greater obedience. He does not condemn us for our immaturity or accuse us for our failures. Instead, He recognizes her budding virtues and calls them forth as though they were realities. He sees our desire for obedience even when it is only in seed form in our hearts. (See Romans 4:17.)

We see our failures and shortcomings, and we may automatically think that God is accusing and condemning us. The devil has deceived us, leading us to attribute to God what is true of himself. Satan, not God, is the accuser of the brethren. God is our affirmer— our encourager. He believes in our sincere desires to obey Him more than we do and calls us forth in ways we would never dream. He says, "I love you! I have great affection for you! I will transform a fervent, immature maiden into My reigning, mature bride."

EMBRACING THE CROSS—
SONG OF SOLOMON 4:6–7

The turning point in the maiden's life comes in chapter 4:

I will go my way to the mountain of myrrh

And to the hill of frankincense.

You are all fair, my love,

And there is no spot in you.

—Song of Solomon 4:6–7, nkjv

She reverses the decision she made in Song of Solomon 2:17, when she refused to go with Him to the mountains. Now she is willing to go to the mountain even if it causes her difficulty, as symbolized by myrrh. Myrrh, which was used in preparing a body for burial, and frankincense, which does not give forth its fragrant perfume until it is burned, were two of the gifts laden with prophetic meaning that were given by the wise men to Jesus at His birth. The gifts spoke prophetically of His suffering and death on the cross. She declares, "I will go my way to the mountain of myrrh." Here, the maiden is speaking figuratively of the suffering and death of her beloved. She is saying what you and I must say if we are to experience greater maturity in the Lord: "I want only to be like You. I will embrace the cross. I will not refuse You again. I will arise and go my way to the mountain of myrrh and the hills of frankincense."

The beautiful words that the Lord had just spoken over her in Song of Solomon 4:1–5 have awakened a new confidence and an unwavering resolve in the maiden's heart to fully obey the Lord even to the point of now going to the mountain.

Some people think the will of God is always hard, but that's not true. Paul testified that the will of God is good, satisfying, and perfect (Rom. 12:2). We find great fulfillment and joy in doing the will of God. On the other hand, there are times when we must say no to the desires of our flesh, times when our own carnal passions conflict with the will of God. At such times we must deny ourselves, and yes, that is difficult.

That is what Jesus meant when He said, "If anyone wishes to come after Me, let him deny himself, and take up his cross daily, and follow Me" (Luke 9:23). He said we cannot be His disciples without doing this. If we want to be co-laborers with Jesus, fulfilling His purposes in the earth, we must step out of the comfort zone and move into the life of faith where our only source is the invisible God and the integrity of His Word.

Did you notice the maiden said, "I will go *my way* to the mountain of myrrh..." (Song of Sol. 4:6, emphasis added)? The cross you embrace will be different from the cross another person is called to embrace. Trying to embrace another's cross may result in legalism. What is an easy yoke of obedience for one believer may become a religious burden for another who embraces what God has not called that believer to.

The grace of God has gifted my life with a passion for intercession. I tried to force that yoke on the members of my church over the years without bearing good fruit. I preached to others that they *must* spend as much time in intercession for revival as I did. They tried to respond, but they became burned-out because they were being pressured to bear my yoke. In the same way, I could not walk in their calling.

You and I must each "go our own ways" to the mountain of myrrh. When God asks us to carry a cross, He also supplies us with grace and a sense of personal conviction that is needed to carry it. The yoke is easy, joyful, and light when He puts it on us (Matt. 11:28–30).

As we begin to know the personality of the Lord, we, like this maiden, feel increasingly secure. "You are a safe God," we will declare. Like the maiden who decides to go up the mountain in obedience to Jesus, we can say to Him, "I'm not afraid anymore. I may lose my job and my house. I may lose my reputation. Nevertheless, I will joyfully go with You to the mountain of myrrh and the hill of frankincense because I trust You, Lord."

The Lord's response to the maiden's new commitment to go to the mountain is dynamic. He proclaims, "You are all fair, my love, and there is no spot in you" (Song of Sol. 4:7).

Remember that the maiden's progression into spiritual maturity in the Song of Solomon still has four chapters to go—the maiden has not fully matured. But the Lord says that there are no spots of compromise in her. He is looking the sincere intention of her heart to obey Him by going up the mountain. Therefore, He exclaims, "There is no spot in you. You are altogether beautiful!"

I can imagine a conversation with our Lord.

"Oh, Lord, I slandered someone today."

"Yes, but when you slandered, you called it sin and cried out for forgiveness, didn't you?"

"Well, yes. But..."

"There's no spot in you, My love. Your heart is reaching out to Mine in sincerity and integrity, and you trust Me."

"Oh, yes. I really want to know You, Lord. I have sought deeper intimacy with You, but I thought You'd be angry with me for slandering."

"I was grieved when you did it, but you repented and called it your enemy."

"Yes, I did. Does that mean You still like me?"

"*Like* you? My heart is overflowing with affection for you!"

"But my life has so many deficiencies, and I continue to make so many mistakes."

"I know that, but as you understand My passionate heart for you, it will bring you to maturity."

Can you sense the renewed commitment to maturity that this conversation between the Lord and His beloved would invoke?

Even when we are weak, even when we fail, the Lord looks at the sincerity and devotion of our hearts and exclaims, "You are so beautiful to Me!" The knowledge that Jesus continues to enjoy us as we are maturing is a foundational truth that empowers us to mature.

EQUIPPING THE SOUL FOR THE TESTS AHEAD—
SONG OF SOLOMON 4:8–10

For the first time in this love song, the maiden is called the "bride." Why? Because she is now maturing to where she functions as His bride. She is now able to walk in greater levels of spiritual warfare. The Lord says to her:

> Come with me from Lebanon, my bride....
> Journey down from the summit...
> From the dens of lions,
> From the mountains of leopards.
>
> —SONG OF SOLOMON 4:8

Lions and leopards are devouring animals. This verse is speaking figuratively of engaging in higher levels of spiritual warfare. Satan is as a roaring lion. When we walk in greater obedience, then we are a greater threat to invade his territory. Therefore, he launches a fiercer counterattack against us.

When I hear people talk about spiritual warfare casually, I think, *Obviously you have never been assaulted by the devil before!* We use the Word of God against Satan, but it is still a very real fight of faith—it is not a game. Sometimes his counterattacks against us can last hours, weeks, or even months. We are confronted with new levels of assault as we ascend the mountain of obedience by leaving the comfortable lower ground. This is costly, but it is worth the trouble. She makes the decision to go up the mountain as she entrusts herself fully to His leadership no matter what the cost.

I have observed this as teams of young people have traveled to Muslim countries on missions trips. Young and excited, they are challenged to minister on the streets to people hostile against the gospel of Jesus. They were unprepared for a new level of spiritual warfare. They came home disillusioned and disappointed because they failed to count the cost.

Taking ground from the enemy and holding on to it requires tenacity and resolution of the heart. Satan pushes, resists, and fights back every step of the way.

When the Lord calls us to skip on mountains and encounter lions and leopards, I am not glib about it. A sobriety comes into my spirit. I know I will need to keep alert with my mind renewed and my thoughts obedient. New levels of obedience bring new levels of spiritual warfare.

THE RAVISHED HEART OF GOD

The Lord cries out to the maiden:

> You have ravished my heart,
> My sister, my spouse;
> You have ravished my heart
> With one look of your eyes.
> —SONG OF SOLOMON 4:9, NKJV

What does it mean to "ravish" the heart?

According to the dictionary, the word *ravish* means "to take away by violence; to overcome with emotions of joy or delight; unusually attractive, pleasing or striking."

The bride had captured His heart, filling it with ecstasy and delight. One look from her eyes had seized His heart and carried it away. "Your love has overwhelmed Me," He exclaims. "You are so strikingly beautiful, so utterly pleasing to Me!"

As the maiden heard the Lord wooing and affirming her, her fears melted away, and she gained courage to follow Him. Remember: all that she has done up to this point is say yes. Yet she has ravished the heart of God with her sincere desire to obey Him. This is what happens to Jesus' heart when we set our souls to fully follow Him at any cost. "You have ravished My heart with one look from your eyes," He exclaims. "Your devotion is beautiful, even delightful to Me."

Did you know that your yes to Christ—your immature but sincere commitment to Him—ravishes His heart? Even though your actions will fall short of your intentions, the devout resolution of your heart overwhelms Him with affection. He yearns for you with a longing for an even more intimate relationship with Him.

It is this revelation of Jesus' ravished heart for us that awakens our hearts to fervency for Him. It ignites holy passion in us. It is His love for us and our response of love and devotion back to Him that act as a breastplate of love, guarding our hearts with holy affections in times of temptation (1 Thess. 5:8).

LEARNING TO DISCERN THE RIGHT VOICE

Some have grown so accustomed to the constant, condemning barrage from the enemy, as well as from their own accusing thoughts, that they do not know what it is like to live without condemnation and rejection clouding their hearts. You may have come to view yourself as a failure who seems worthless, but that is not the way the Lord sees you.

I have a pastor friend who fell into immorality after fifteen years of fruitful ministry. For the next five years, he could only imagine God as being angry with him. He could only think of God as judging him. Through it all he continued to lead people to the Lord and brought deliverance to others. He spoke of God's love and deliverance for others. However, for the longest time he could only think of God as judging him. Through personal counseling times and hearing the Word and believing it, he began to see himself as God saw him—forgiven, loved, and even enjoyed by God.

As we set our soul to follow Him at any cost, we begin to understand that one loving glance really seizes His heart. "You have ravished My heart with one look from your eyes!" He exclaims. "You are lovely to Me and a source of delight to My heart!"

Every time Satan comes to weight down your heart with his lies, speak what the Word says back to him. The next time your own heart points a merciless, judgmental finger at your own failure, listen to the loving voice of Jesus as declared in His Word that says, "We are pleasing and beautiful to Him. Yes, we have ravished His heart!"

When you hear the affirming words of your Beloved, do not open your mouth to protest. Accept them. Believe them. They're really true. His desire is to unveil His heart to you, as we will see next.

CHAPTER II

THE SECRET GARDEN

The Lord has revealed His ravished heart to His bride, but He has much more to say to her. Aware that the bride is not yet ready for the critical tests that still lie in her future, the Lord continues to affirm the bride, expressing His great affection for her.

This is a very important spiritual principle that has application for you and me as believers. The knowledge of God's affection prepares us to experience His fullness and to remain faithful to Him in times of persecution and testing.

EQUIPPING AND CALLING FORTH INTO INCREASING FULLNESS—SONG OF SOLOMON 4:10-12

In the Song of Solomon, the Lord lavishes His love upon His bride as He describes her qualities. He specifically describes how lovely her thoughts, words, and deeds are to Him:

> How much better than wine is your love,
> And the scent of your perfumes
> Than all spices!
> Your lips, O my spouse,
> Drip as the honeycomb...
> And the fragrance of your garments
> Is like the fragrance of Lebanon.

A garden enclosed
Is my sister, my spouse,
A spring shut up,
A fountain sealed.

—Song of Solomon 4:10–12, nkjv

Earlier, the bride told the Lord that His love for her was better than wine (Song of Sol. 1:2). Now He gazes longingly and tenderly at her and reverses her statement by saying, "How much better than wine is your love."

Jesus declares that our love for Him is better than wine—it is better than all the kingdoms of the world, better than all the glorious works of His hands. Truly, the heart of Jesus is utterly ravished by the resolute heart, the loving abandonment of His church for Him.

The beloved finds wonderful delight in his beautiful bride in three ways—her perfume, the sweetness of her lips, the fragrance of her garments. There is a symbolic meaning here for you and me.

The fragrance of godly thoughts and prayers before the throne

The scent of the bride's perfume can represent her inner thought life, which emanates as a lovely fragrance to the Lord. God hears the secret cry of our spirits that no one else hears, and it ascends as a beautiful perfume before Him. God sees the secret intentions of our hearts as we long to please Him, even when we come up short.

In John's vision recorded in the Book of Revelation, there were golden bowls full of incense carried by the twenty-four elders and the four creatures. These bowls were "full of incense, which are the prayers of the saints" (Rev. 5:8).

The cry of the saints to the Lord is as fragrant incense to Him. David said, "You number my wanderings; put my tears into Your bottle; are they not in Your book?" (Ps. 56:8, nkjv). David was weeping over his own failings. Our tears of repentance and sorrow are precious to the Lord.

Instead of condemning ourselves and other Christians who fall, we must realize that our tears are precious to God. When we get to heaven, I wouldn't be surprised if a conversation much like this takes place:

"O Lord, You know I sinned and failed You so many times as I served You on earth."

"Yes, that's true," the Lord will respond. "But what you didn't realize was that I heard the moans and cries of your spirit when you failed Me. I saw every tear as it trickled down your cheek."

"How could I have been so confused? Half the time I wasn't sure if You loved me or not. Sometimes I wasn't even sure if I loved You."

"I knew that," He may say. "I could see your confusion. I could feel your pain. But even in your darkest, most difficult hours, I saw a flame of love for Me deep in your spirit."

Edifying words and righteous deeds

What are the milk, honey, and fragrant garments the beloved mentions? Just as milk and honey help nurture bodies, the lips dripping with milk and honey are the bride's edifying, life-giving words that nurture the faith of the young instead of accusing, slandering, criticizing, and finding fault.

> Your lips, O My spouse,
> Drip as the honeycomb;
> Honey and milk are under your tongue;
> And the fragrance of your garments
> Is like the fragrance of Lebanon.
>
> —Song of Solomon 4:11, nkjv

The Lord said that the maiden's lips were like milk and honey. In other words, the maiden's words were dripping with that which brought life and nurtured the faith of the young. So many slander and criticize God's immature saints. However, the maiden spoke of God's tenderness to those who sought to walk in His ways. Her fragrant garments are her righteous deeds of service. The nineteenth chapter of Revelation describes the bride ready for the marriage to the Lamb. Of her garments it says:

> And it was given to her to clothe herself in fine linen, bright and clean; for the fine linen is the righteous acts of the saints.
>
> —REVELATION 19:8

When the intention of our hearts is to be a servant, our service exudes a beautiful fragrance in the presence of God (2 Cor. 2:15–16). Our intent to lay our lives down for the Lord, crucifying our own self-centeredness, ascends like a pleasing perfume to the Lord.

Your spirit is reserved for Him

Next, the Lord compares His bride to "a garden enclosed" or "a spring shut up and a fountain sealed."

> A garden enclosed
> Is my sister, my spouse,
> A spring shut up,
> A fountain sealed.
>
> —SONG OF SOLOMON 4:12, NKJV

The common gardens in the ancient world were open so that even the animals could drink from their springs. The result was that the animals polluted the clean waters. However, the garden that belonged to a king was enclosed. In other words, it was a private garden reserved for the king's pleasure only. A king's garden was his special place of pleasure and rest. It was not designed for economic productivity, as a large field would be. The king would not count how many bushels of roses he harvested from his garden each year. No, he would go to his garden to enjoy it, to be refreshed by its beauty.

When I traveled to Vienna, Austria, I enjoyed visiting the Hapsburg Palace. It has a magnificent garden that has been maintained over the years strictly for the pleasure of the king and his family. Completely walled off from the rest of the palace, the garden is filled with tens of thousands of beautiful flowers.

The Lord is asking you and me to be His locked garden, a place in which He has personal delight.

The heart of the bride is not open to the polluting spirit of the world. Her heart is as a locked garden, sealed for her beloved King only, one in which the gates are not left standing ajar so strangers or animals could wander in. There is no "For Sale" sign posted. She continually says no to immorality, pride, and greed. Her gifts and anointing are not to be sold or prostituted. They are used only for the pleasure of her beloved King.

SUBMITTING TO HIS DEALINGS—
SONG OF SOLOMON 4:16–5:1

As the Lord lavishes His love upon the maiden, she breaks out with one of the great prayers of the Song of Solomon:

> Awake, O north wind,
> And come, O south!
> Blow upon my garden,
> That its spices may flow out.
> Let my beloved come to his garden
> And eat its pleasant fruits.
>
> —SONG OF SOLOMON 4:16, NKJV

The north wind communicates the cold, bitter winds of winter, and the south wind is the warm, refreshing wind that comes during the sowing of the seed and the summer season of growth. The bride asks for both winds. She asks for the harsh north wind to blow on her in order to reveal what is in her heart, but she also asks for the blessing and refreshing of the south wind.

We never outgrow our need for the south winds of blessing. I have seen hyperspiritual people who thought they were more committed to God than He was to them. I've heard them pray, "O God, forget the blessings. I just want the purging and purifying."

I'm not remotely tempted to tell God to forget the south winds. I love the blessings that flow in with the south winds. Sometimes I reverse the order: "Send the south winds, God! (And, oh, by the way, if You must, then send a few north winds, too.)" Unlike me, the bride had it in right order.

When we can ask for both winds—His dealings and His blessings—we are saying, "You love me so much; therefore, I know it's safe to be in Your hands. I trust You. I'm not afraid of the difficult circumstances of the north winds. I know You will only give me what benefits my life in Christ. You have guarded my every step."

We must not confuse the north wind with the attack of the devil. We never invite his attack. That is absolute foolishness, for we must always resist the devil and his onslaught and attacks.

The bride says, "Make *my* garden breathe out fragrance....May my beloved come into *his* garden and eat its choice fruits" (Song of Sol. 4:16, emphasis added). She wants her beloved to get his full inheritance from her life. It is a dynamic time in our life when we become focused on the Lord's inheritance in us, and not just our inheritance in Him. In other words, what He receives from us, not just what we receive from Him. The prayer of the lovesick worshiper cries out, "Come into every area of my heart, Lord. Receive my obedience as pleasurable fruit that I offer to You." When we trust our Beloved, we are not afraid to pray: "I want my heart to be yoked with Your heart. Your inheritance in me is the most important thing in my life. Therefore, awake, O north wind!"

ENDURING THE REJECTION OF OTHER BELIEVERS—
SONG OF SOLOMON 5:6–8

Now comes the maiden's ultimate twofold test: the Lord withholds His presence, and even His people reject her:

> I opened for my beloved,
> But my beloved had turned away and was gone.
> My heart leaped up when he spoke.
> I sought him, but I could not find him;
> I called him, but he gave me no answer.
> The watchmen who went about the city found me.
> They struck me, they wounded me;
> The keepers of the walls took my veil away from me.
> I charge you, O daughters of Jerusalem,
> If you find my beloved,
> That you tell him I am lovesick!
> —SONG OF SOLOMON 5:6–8, NKJV

This is the second time that the Lord left the maiden in this love song. In chapter 3, He left as an expression of divine discipline so as to draw her into obedience. This time He has withdrawn His presence in order to test her.

Sooner or later, you and I will also confront this twofold test.

The first test is the loss of the conscious presence of God that so satisfies her soul. She said, "My beloved turned away and was gone." This is a temporary test. This withdrawing of His presence was not due to her disobedience but rather because of her obedience and desire for full maturity.

Does she serve God for the good feelings that she gets from His presence, or is she willing to be His without any conditions whatsoever? Jesus does not simply want to be a stepping-stone to better things. He is to be our magnificent obsession.

It is as if the Lord is saying, "Let Me ask you, My bride: Am I only a source for your spiritual satisfaction, or am I the consuming reason for your very life? Am I a means to your end, or am I the very end goal of your life? Will you serve Me if there are no spiritual feelings? When My discernible presence is gone, will you still say, 'I am Your loving bondservant'?"

The second test occurs when the watchmen or the leadership in the church strike and wound her and then take her covering away. When we stand for truth, sometimes even the Lord's own servants will strike us. We must endure the misunderstanding and rejection of other believers.

Have fellow Christians—people to whom you have committed yourself—ever misunderstood you and risen up against you? For no justifiable reason, have they ever turned against you, wounded you, and stripped you of your honor, place, and function among other Christians? Do you know what it is to stand bleeding and naked, feeling as if God Himself has left you?

It appeared as if she lost her entire inheritance in Him. She was stripped of the sense of His presence and of His favor in the church. But like Job, this maiden did not know that the test she was experiencing would be only for a season. In the midst of pain, she was maturing in the Spirit. It is as if we can hear her proclaiming, "I'm not in it for myself anymore. I'm in it for You, my beloved King. You are my passion and portion."

Next, we find her speaking with the daughters of Jerusalem, the spiritually immature believers: "If you find my Beloved, tell Him I'm not angry. I'm not offended because He withdrew and let this happen to me. I love Him. I'm lovesick, not angry."

When the Lord sees that response of love in us, even while we are walking in the midst of the fiery test, He exclaims, "Yes! That is the heart of My true bride!"

In my opinion, Song of Solomon 5:10–16 is the most outstanding statement of love in the Word of God. It is written in symbolic language, but when understood, no passage outshines this one in expressing loving adoration to Jesus.

The maiden stands stripped and wounded before her accusers, and she answers, "My beloved is dazzling and ruddy, outstanding among ten thousand" (Song of Sol. 5:10). She then proceeds to describe some of the precious attributes of her beloved king in symbolic language, mentioning His head, hair, eyes, cheeks, lips, hands, body, legs, countenance, and mouth. She praises the excellence of who he is, the infinite loveliness of everything he does. "He's dazzling!…This is my beloved and this is my friend," she cries (vv. 10, 16).

She focuses on the reality of his majestic personality. It is the knowledge of her beloved that stabilizes her. She is overflowing in worship as she declares the splendor of his personhood through these ten attributes. Her response is not one of offense with him for withdrawing his presence and allowing rejection from others. Rather, she magnifies his greatness as one who is lovesick (v. 8).

BRINGING OTHERS INTO INTIMACY WITH HIM—
SONG OF SOLOMON 6:1

What is the response of others when they see you standing utterly resolute in your commitment and unwavering in your affection for Jesus even in the midst of suffering, rejection, and persecution? What is their response when they see that price is no object for you and that you are totally committed to Jesus regardless of what comes your way?

Where has your beloved gone,
O most beautiful among women?
Where has your beloved turned,
That we may seek him with you?

—Song of Solomon 6:1

They cry out, "We want what you have in Him. We want Him, too!" As the Holy Spirit reveals more and more of the personality of Jesus to our hearts, our commitment will deepen, and we will inspire even more to passionately follow Jesus. Some of these newly impassioned believers will be sixteen years old, some forty-five, and some ninety-two. Some will be truck drivers, and some chief executive officers of corporations. God is raising up a company of believers whose impassioned devotion to Him will inspire many.

WHAT CAN SUBDUE THE HEART OF GOD?

Like the beloved in the Song of Solomon, our Beloved sees when believers respond to the brutal tests of life with adoration and abandoned worship. He is utterly overwhelmed by His bride's devotion to Him:

O my love, you are as beautiful as Tirzah,
Lovely as Jerusalem,
Awesome as an army with banners!
Turn your eyes away from me,
For they have overcome me.

—Song of Solomon 6:4–5, NKJV

"Turn your eyes away from Me," our Beloved cries, "*for they have overcome Me!*" Think of it! The God of heaven overwhelmed. No army, no principality, no power in heaven or earth can conquer Him who measured the waters in the hollow of His hand and marked off the heavens with the span of His fingers. The God who calculated the dust of the earth, weighed the mountains in a balance. The God who calls all the stars by name. Only one thing can conquer God's heart: the affectionate love of His people who say yes to Him in times of testing.

CONTINUING IN THE PROGRESSION OF HOLY PASSION

We have seen in the beautiful Song of Solomon that as our Beloved reveals the depths of His personality to us, that revelation enables us to stand firm in times of trouble and testing. As we begin to comprehend His majestic beauty, we are not offended when we do not understand the way He is leading us. Even in the most difficult, trying times, our hearts overflow with adoration for our Beloved.

The Song of Solomon reveals some additional truths about the believer's affectionate relationship with Jesus.

After we have stood true to Jesus in the face of lying accusations and rejection, He will validate us (Song of Sol. 6:4–13). We will no longer live for our pleasure, but for His pleasure alone (Song of Sol. 7:1–10). As we labor with Him to reap the harvest, other believers will be inspired to love Jesus as we do (Song of Sol. 7:11; 8:5). He will set the flaming seal of His love upon our hearts (vv. 6–7). The devotion and passion that Christ has for us will bring us to full maturity and overflowing passion for Him. Thus, He will receive His full inheritance from our lives (vv. 8–14).

We are Jesus' bride, the one the Father gave Him as His most prized possession!

THE SONG OF OUR BELOVED

Let me encourage you to take the Song of Solomon and turn its verses into devotional meditation. This beautiful song of divine love is breathtaking when we begin to understand the prophetic nature of its words. They are life changing when we realize our Beloved is also speaking them over us, affirming and drawing forth qualities not yet fully developed in our lives. Oh, that God would give us new eyes to see His affectionate, yearning heart for us while we are still growing, still failing, still weak in so many ways.

Never allow the truths in God's beautiful love song to be forgotten and fade away in your heart. Cherish the message of His love for you. Jesus enjoys you and continually affirms you, even in your imperfection and immaturity. As we understand that He is ravished with our love, then our heart is filled with courage and confidence. Understanding the affectionate personality of God equips us to wage war against the enemy and to demolish the lying, accusing strongholds he has erected in our minds. Resting in the certain knowledge of God's ravished heart enables us to stand unoffended and unshaken in times of pressure and rejection.

As you have seen in the Song of Solomon, God pursues you with a relentless, infinite love. Do not let this truth grow cold in your heart. God is not some mystical, nebulous force that loves the masses but not individuals, whose love is focused on vast populations but not on individual people. You serve a loving God whose heart is ravished by the beauty of your sincere, devoted heart. You are so beautiful to Him! I believe that in the years to come the Lord will release more revelation of Himself through the Song of Solomon.

God, may You use the Song of Solomon to release a thousand songs through a thousand languages. May Your message of love be sung fresh every time! May the revelation of Your ravished heart bring Your bride to full maturity.

CHAPTER 12

TWELVE EXPRESSIONS OF GOD'S BEAUTY

W e have seen in the last few chapters how God sees us and relates to us in our journey toward Him. How are we to return these affections to Him? More importantly, what is it about God that inspires us to pursue Him with the radical abandonment of the bride in the Song of Solomon? In exploring the passages in the Scripture most focused on the subject of God's beauty, I summarized this wonderful topic into twelve different categories, or more accurately, twelve expressions of God's beauty. These summaries are certainly not exhaustive, but rather form the most obvious points that could only be properly revealed in a book dedicated to the purpose.

EXPRESSION 1:
THE BEAUTY OF THE LIGHT OF GOD'S BEING

God's beauty is seen in His light. In a literal sense, it is the light that emanates out of Him, the colors and brilliant glory that pour out from His being. God has given us a hint, a mere breath of knowledge, to see the dazzling brilliance and the many colors that radiate from Him. Paul says that we now see dimly in a mirror (1 Cor. 13:12), and though we do not see every outline perfectly reflected in this dim beholding, we see enough to gain that titillating first taste to direct our minds during prayer toward God on His throne.

In Revelation 4:3 (TLB), John focuses on three of the colors that he sees in his glorious throne room experience, colors he sees woven in God's own being. He sees the brightness of diamonds, the deep shining red ruby, and the seven colors of the rainbow dominated by an emerald green. Just as the psalmist says that God covers Himself "with light as a garment" (Ps. 104:2, NKJV), so we gain a clearer view of this light in which the Almighty wraps Himself and its many colors.

Peter described this same light as "marvelous," and when we stand before the Lord we will assuredly marvel at the beauty and majesty of God's garment and light. But even greater, Peter goes on to assure us that we are called into this light (1 Pet. 2:9). We will experience it forever and ever, and even now, when we meditate on the Word, when we pray or worship, we experience small measures of this light. In the same way, when I quiet myself and focus on the Holy Spirit living within me, gazing upon His brilliance, this light sometimes touches me just a little.

Paul discusses this light as well, describing God the Father as living in "unapproachable light" that nobody can see (1 Tim. 6:16). This is not an effort to distance Himself from us, but rather to protect us from the far-greater brilliance of His being. We are welcomed to come close before the Lord, but to come before Him in His unveiled majesty would surely overwhelm us. To realize that He chooses dazzling light to shield His actual being gives us an idea of how magnificent He truly is.

Our capacities to comprehend and enjoy God will increase throughout all eternity—even the capacities of our resurrected bodies will increase. It is not a question of having the right to approach God, for we have been given this glorious right because of God's righteousness that Jesus provided for us (2 Cor. 5:17–21). We need supernatural capacities to relate to the God who possesses such majesty that the very heaven and earth flee from His presence (Rev. 20:11).

Isaiah 6 speaks of the high-ranking angels, seraphim, as bowing down and astounded as God continuously reveals more of His majesty to them. They cover their eyes because they are so overwhelmed by what they see. Their cry of "Holy, holy, holy!" is a proclamation of God's transcendent beauty, bursting unbidden from their hearts. Not until they have settled that revelation—or at least partly recovered from it—do they peer out from beneath their wings again, only to be overcome yet again with another wave of God's glory as it crashes over them. This in itself is a witness to us that we shall never cease to be overwhelmed at the brightness of God's glory. This astounding God who clothes Himself in blinding light to protect us from His limitless glory is the One who calls Himself our Father.

EXPRESSION 2:
THE BEAUTY OF JESUS' RESURRECTED BODY

God's beauty is manifested in Jesus' physical resurrected body. Isaiah prophesied that to see Jesus in His glorious resurrected body at the time of His Second Coming will be overwhelming (Isa. 4:2). His resurrected body is powerful and glorious. It is all beautiful. The psalmist cries, "You are fairer than the sons of men" (Ps. 45:2, NKJV). More than all the sons of men in history, Jesus is more beautiful than any other human being that ever walked on the earth or on the streets of gold in heaven. Isaiah described Jesus in His glorified and resurrected body in a very different way than he described Him veiling His beauty while on the earth during His earthly ministry (Isa. 53:2–3). During that time, men were not to be awed by His physical presence, but rather by His love, meekness, and righteousness.

Even in Jesus' glorified body, He can choose to manifest His glory in varying degrees according to the circumstance. For example, when Mary Magdalene went to the tomb on Resurrection morning, she mistook Him for a gardener because He was veiling His resurrected glory. He then had the power to shake the foundations of the earth by His very appearance, yet He chose to restrain His power. Likewise, when He cooked breakfast for seven of the disciples by the Sea of Galilee, He restrained His glory. Or when He encountered two disciples on the road to Emmaus, they talked face-to-face with the Son of God without recognizing Him. They would recount how their hearts burned just from their speech with Him, but their eyes did not see His glory.

John's heavenly vision in Revelation 1 caused him, as Jesus' closest friend, to fall like a dead man before His splendor and majesty. In Revelation 21–22 we see that the glory of the resurrected Jesus will light up the New Jerusalem and the entire world. Even John's fearsome encounter was far from the fullness of Jesus' glory. When Jesus said, "I am the light of the world" (John 8:12), He meant that He was more than just "the source of truth during this age." He is the source of the actual light for the New Jerusalem for eternity (Rev. 21:11, 23–24).

Jesus' very garments possess supernatural qualities. When Isaiah saw Jesus marching through the land to the Battle of Jerusalem at the time of the Second Coming (Isa. 63:1), he said that Jesus' clothing was glorious. John saw that Jesus' very eyes have fire in them, the penetrating fire that burns with zeal and passion. His voice is compared to a trumpet. His white hair, like the Father's white hair in Daniel 7, speaks of His infinite wisdom and eternal nature. The words of His mouth are like a sharp, two-edged sword (Rev. 1:12–18). Jesus' face shines like the sun in its strength and will be the very weapon He uses to consume His enemies (2 Thess. 2:8). The Antichrist, who boasted of Jesus' defeat, will crumble to nothing in the moment that he beholds Jesus at the Second Coming. One breath from Jesus and this wicked man of lawlessness will be defeated. The face of Jesus is holy and powerful, yet inviting and warm to those who receive the grace of God. The smile on His face, the warmth of His eyes, and the brightness of His countenance are filled with beauty as they conquer God's people with love.

EXPRESSION 3:
THE BEAUTY OF THE MUSIC OF GOD

The most common expression of entertainment throughout all history is music. Though it can be used by the devil in a negative way, it was created by God to bless His people. The reason why we love music is because the human spirit is musical. God simply created us that way. God invented music and created us with a musical spirit because it releases His beauty.

God's heavenly throne is surrounded by music because His beauty is revealed in His music. Jesus is an incredible singer, songwriter, and musician. Zephaniah says that when God is in our midst, He will rejoice over His people with singing (Zeph. 3:17, NKJV). Psalm 22:3 says that God inhabits the praises of His people—that when He sings, He actually lives and expresses His authority through the songs that He gives His people. Likewise, Hebrews 2:12 portrays Jesus as singing in the midst of His people by the spirit of prophecy that rests on them. David, the man after God's own heart, was a forerunner and a picture of Jesus in many ways. The great musician and psalmist reflected Jesus' anointing in music.

The Holy Spirit Himself is filled with music. Heaven is filled with music that comes out of God's being. All heaven is filled with beautiful music that flows out of God's heart.

The harpists that surround God's throne (Rev. 14:2–3) reveal much about God's personality, especially in the way that His music mingles with the voices from His throne and the sound of many waters and thunder. God's musical voice is powerful (Ps. 29:4). It releases the activity of the Holy Spirit in heaven just as it did on earth in Genesis 1.

God's voice is strong and beautiful and is filled with majesty. It is musical, and above all, it is authoritative; His musical voice fills heaven with beautiful melodies.

Mighty voices proceed from God's throne (Rev. 4:5), which include the Holy Spirit's voice as well as God Himself speaking. The implication from the Book of Revelation is that the voices from the throne originate in God and are often musical in nature. These voices are the sound of the author of music.

EXPRESSION 4:
THE BEAUTY OF THE FRAGRANCE OF CHRIST

All heaven is filled with the fragrances that come from God. The psalmist referred to the various fragrances with which Jesus' garments were scented (Ps. 45:8). We can only guess how these perfumes and wonderful scents will be used on different celebratory occasions in heaven, or how they will draw our attention to associated ideas or events from the past. Every facet of Jesus' character is like an infusion of perfume. I think that His perfume is released when He shows forth His character in different settings.

The bride in the Song of Solomon, in asking her beloved Messiah to come quickly, beckons Him to the mountains of spice. This is a reference to Jesus' throne of glory (Matt. 19:28; 25:31). The bride describes Jesus' throne as the "mountain of spices" because His throne will be drenched in divine fragrances and perfumes. In eternity, Jesus will actually possess literal fragrance.

The bride continues to say, "Because of the fragrance of Jesus' good perfumes, Your name is like perfume that is poured forth." (See Song of Solomon 1:3.) Another phrase she uses is, "Your character is like perfume poured forth." Paul said to the Corinthians, "We are to God the fragrance of Christ" (2 Cor. 2:15, NKJV).

Even today in our natural bodies, smell plays a huge part in regards to memory, and a faint whiff of a familiar odor can conjure up a plethora of thoughts, positive or negative. Imagine this sense redeemed, when the fragrance of God hangs thick in the air, ever changing, bringing our attention to whatever aspect of Himself He wants to share.

EXPRESSION 5:

THE BEAUTY OF GOD'S THRONE

The beauty of God is seen in the magnificent scene arrayed before His throne, drawing in the light and the music, the fragrance and the splendor, the seraphim, saints, elders, and all the heavenly assembly. No doubt you have seen St. Peter's Square in Vatican City in Rome where the pope delivers his orations to hundreds of thousands of devotees. Picture a heavenly pavilion that spaciously accommodates billions of saints and angels. It is called "the sea of glass, like crystal" and is covered in winds, music, fire, and perfume (Rev. 4:6; 15:2). The queen of Sheba's utter astonishment at the matchless extent of Solomon's royal court is a picture of the complete inadequacy of any earthly thing to compare to God's heavenly court.

God's throne is His governmental center of the universe. "Honor and majesty are before Him, strength and beauty are in His sanctuary" (Ps. 96:6). It is here that God receives honor— and dispenses it as well. It is here that we find the supernatural expressions of God's wisdom and power. Ezekiel and John were both at a loss for words to describe it adequately. All of God's authority comes from this one place, and the highest beauty of God exists at this royal court, to be released throughout the eternal city and the earth.

EXPRESSION 6:
THE BEAUTY OF GOD'S ETERNAL CITY

God established the eternal city as full of beauty (Rev. 21:2–22:5). The New Jerusalem, created as an extension and an expression of His heart, is the city that the saints will inherit.

God is the author and architect of the New Jerusalem in all of its splendid design and unimaginable beauty. From the landscaping of trees and gardens, to the rivers and ponds, to the color, music, and fragrance that will fill it, this city will literally embody every facet of God's personality. For those who are well versed in interior design, this city that is illuminated entirely by the brilliance of Jesus will be lit to enhance mood and atmosphere to the apex of perfection and desirability. That God should have created us to appreciate light on so many levels in our homes when He plans all the while to live with us in perfect light is stunning.

EXPRESSION 7:
THE BEAUTY OF GOD'S PERSONALITY

The beauty of God's personality is perhaps one of the greatest and most important expressions to understand. I explore the attributes of God's emotions and the revelation we gain through them in more detail in chapter sixteen. When we understand His emotions, we have insight into why God does the things He does. We are able to peer into the strong desire for His people that burns within Him

(John 17). We are able to see just how full of delight, pleasure, and gladness God is.

Moses had a glimpse at the glad nature of God when he recorded that "the LORD your God will make you abound in all the work of your hand.... For the LORD will again rejoice over you for good as He rejoiced over your fathers" (Deut. 30:9, NKJV). The gladness and joy of the Lord are central to all He does. He really enjoys His people and even takes pleasure in them (Ps. 149:4).

Likewise, the holiness of God's personality expresses His beauty. His holiness is reliable and unchanging, expressing His highest virtues. How terrible it would be if God's mercies were arbitrary, or if His standards of holiness changed over time. His holiness is perfectly steadfast and consistent.

EXPRESSION 8:
THE BEAUTY OF GOD'S TRANSCENDENT POWER

Standing alone, God's power is beautiful. The heavens declare the beauty of the Lord (Ps. 19:1–6), and the Holy Spirit is the designer of the heavens whose beauty astounds us (Job 26:13).

Just think of the hundred billion stars in the Milky Way galaxy alone, and that is not taking into account the other thousands of galaxies yet unknown. This puts God's power and wisdom in perspective.

The beauty of His power is readily apparent. Think of how each snowflake is unique; no two are exactly alike. Just gaze at the majestic mountains or how the sun rises and sets each day and the awesome power it supplies. Think of how God has synchronized the oceans' tides with the gravitational pull of the moon in perfect harmony, and you will be getting just a tiny glimpse into His glorious transcendent power.

It is easy to see why the maiden in the Song of Solomon describes Jesus' leadership as "finest gold." "By Him all things were created that are in heaven and that are on earth" (Col. 1:16, NKJV).

EXPRESSION 9:
THE BEAUTY OF GOD'S LEADERSHIP

Closely linked to the beauty of God's power are His infinite wisdom and perfect knowledge as seen in His brilliant plans for human history. In the same way that fine works of art and science are admired in deference to the mind behind the feat, the orchestration of all history, dovetailing to form the greatest story ever told, shows us that God has a most beautiful mind. When the saints stand before the Lord in Revelation 15:3, they shall cry, "Your plans and Your leadership make us marvel!" God's fantastic story line for human history was ordained by God from the beginning, and it will continue throughout eternity. Truly, His wisdom is great and marvelous.

EXPRESSION 10:
THE BEAUTY OF THE HOLY SPIRIT'S MINISTRY
AND IMPARTATION

The Holy Spirit's ministry is seen in its finest before the throne of God, where we see the seven torches of Holy Spirit fire burning beside the sea of fiery glass, both before the throne of God (Rev. 4:5–6). The magnificent flame beheld in the seraphim, the burning ones, is the power of the Holy Spirit's fire. They reveal four different faces of God and give us insight into the way the Spirit works in the lives of God's people. In like impartation, God strengthens, renews, and transforms His enemies into His beloved servants who reflect His beauty.

EXPRESSION 11:
THE BEAUTY OF GOD'S PARTNERSHIP

The indescribable beauty of God is seen in His desire to share His reign with us forever. Solomon said, "An excellent wife is the crown of her husband" (Prov. 12:4). Out of humanity, those who were formerly His enemies, God has raised up a bride. He has both cleansed and exalted her. He has qualified His bride to reign with Him, making her excellent and one who shines forth the very beauty of Jesus.

We are given the incredible privilege of representing God forever to all of creation as His priests. It is through us that God's heart toward His creation will be expressed and through us that this infinite beauty will be conducted. We cannot help but declare to Him, "It is so kind of You to choose us as Your priestly representatives." It is part of His beauty that He would give us His very own glory.

EXPRESSION 12:
THE BEAUTY OF GOD'S WORD

The Word of the Lord is wise and pure and is altogether righteous. When it touches our spirit, it is sweeter than honey (Ps. 19:8–10). This beautiful Word will not simply fade into obscurity or become relegated to a historical textbook on "the way things used to be." Rather, the Word of God will be giving us significant revelation a billion years from now—the same Books of Acts, Romans, Isaiah, Genesis, and Revelation will be relevant forever. The bride's exclamation that His "mouth is most sweet. Yes, You are altogether lovely" speaks of the Word of His mouth that is sweet to our spirit. This same sweet Word will excite our spirits forever.

CHAPTER 13

THE KNOWLEDGE OF GOD TO THE ENDS OF THE EARTH

All nations will hear the great message of the gospel that Christ died for them and that He is coming back to rule the earth. They will also see the demonstration of His glory manifested in the lives of people walking in passion for Jesus. "This gospel of the kingdom will be preached in all the world as a witness to all the nations, and then the end will come" (Matt. 24:14, NKJV).

> I looked, and behold, a great multitude which no one could number, of all nations, tribes, peoples, and tongues, standing before the throne and before the Lamb, clothed with white robes.... "These are the ones who come out of the great tribulation, and washed their robes and made them white in the blood of the Lamb."
>
> —REVELATION 7:9, 14, NKJV

Paul's description of the glorious church is the clearest and most specific passage emphasizing this aspect of God's purpose for the church in the generation that the Lord returns.

> He gave some as apostles, and some as prophets, and some as evangelists, and some as pastors and teachers, for the equipping of the saints for the work of service, to the building up of the body of Christ; *until* we all attain to the unity of the faith, and of

the knowledge of the Son of God, to a mature man, to the measure of the stature which belongs to the fulness of Christ.

—EPHESIANS 4:11–13, EMPHASIS ADDED

When Paul says, "Attain to the…knowledge of the Son of God," he is not referring to the initial saving knowledge of the gospel. Paul is writing to the believers at Ephesus, assuring them that one of the purposes of the church's ministry is to lead people into an experiential knowledge of Jesus. In other words, into intimacy with Jesus. These verses state very clearly that the church will attain to three specific things:

1. Unity of faith
2. Intimate knowledge of Jesus
3. Spiritual maturity

God's purposes with the church in this age are not complete until these three things take place: unity, intimacy, and maturity. The church will be restored to these three dimensions before the Lord comes back to take His bride unto Himself. The revived and restored church will be a significant "sign of the times" of Jesus' coming. God has been restoring various truths to the church for many years. I believe our generation is witnessing a new acceleration in God's activity of restoration. Part of the church's restoration includes ministries that will function for the equipping and building up of the church into these three dimensions. Throughout church history and the common course of Christianity, we have seen some measure of these ministries wherever sincere people have been functioning in the body of Christ. But we are about to see them come forth in maturity on a worldwide scale.

That He might sanctify and cleanse her with the washing of water by the word, that He might present her to Himself a glorious church, not having spot or wrinkle or any such thing, but that she should be holy and without blemish.

—Ephesians 5:26–27, nkjv

How is the restoration of the church to come about? How will the redeemed be filled with the knowledge of God and consumed with affection for Jesus? "The zeal of the Lord of hosts will accomplish this" (Isa. 9:7). Before the Lord returns, He will openly manifest a new measure of His zeal in and through the church.

RESTORING JESUS AS THE FOCAL POINT IN THE CHURCH

The church has focused on many of the different benefits of redemption—forgiveness, outreach, healing, power, wholeness, and increased blessing on our circumstances. The Holy Spirit will jealously insist that the magnificent Personhood of Jesus become the primary focal point in the body of Christ. The church knows Jesus as Savior but does not know Him intimately as an infinitely glorious Person. The church has not experienced the excellencies of His perfection. In many ways Jesus is still a stranger in His own house. Jesus spoke with His disciples concerning the zeal that the Holy Spirit has to make Him known:

If I go, I will send Him to you....He shall glorify Me; for He shall take of Mine, and shall disclose it to you.

—John 16:7, 14

The Holy Spirit has an intense agenda to fill the church with the revelation of Jesus. At the top of His list of divine activities and responsibilities is to glorify Jesus Christ by empowering God's people with holy affection for Jesus. When Jesus is revealed in His glory, a new hunger for purity results. Isaiah saw the Lord lifted up and cried out for his own cleansing; then he offered himself for any service that the Lord wanted, crying out, "Here am I. Send me!"

I saw the Lord sitting on a throne, high and lifted up.... Above it stood seraphim.... And one cried to another and said: "Holy, holy, holy is the LORD of hosts; the whole earth is full of His glory!"... So I said: "Woe is me, for I am undone! Because I am a man of unclean lips... for my eyes have seen the King, the LORD of hosts."... Also I heard the voice of the Lord, saying: "Whom shall I send, and who will go for Us?" Then I said, "Here am I! Send me."

—ISAIAH 6:1–8, NKJV

Jesus is not coming for a church that's gritting her teeth, struggling to stay free from sin, secretly wishing she could indulge in a little immorality. No, Jesus is coming for a church utterly devoted to Him—one that is free on the inside. The greatest motivation for obedience comes as we encounter more revelation of who Jesus is.

PREPARING FOR THE COMING REVIVAL

So many Christians today are content to sit behind the church's stained-glass windows in their own little comfort zones, unconcerned with the disastrous plight of unbelievers outside the door of the church. Many believers are disillusioned and are, therefore, preoccupied with their own personal concerns rather than being diligent in the prayer room for revival and the outpouring of the Holy Spirit to meet the needs of the multitudes in the nations.

Too many today are focused primarily on seeking to find the good life for themselves. They are seeking Jesus as the way to make life happier. This is the extent of their focus. They are unwilling to take risks or to stretch beyond their comfort level to take the love of God to those who know nothing of it.

Why are we Christians lolling around passively in our own little comfort zones, tuning out the Holy Spirit, neglecting the place of prayer and the Word of God? Why are we ignoring God's promptings to reach out to the lost and needy? Why do we compromise and backslide? The body of Christ is preoccupied with entertainment as she is held in bondage with a self-centered gospel. This leaves her powerless and filled with strife and petty arguments. We are spiritually bored and shallow because we do not yet have a vision to cry out for a new and fresh encounter with Jesus, one that continues far beyond a one-time experience.

I believe a great revival is coming, as well as a great harvest of souls. Hundreds of millions of new converts will be added to the church across the nations. God's people must be ready, since we are the ones who will be caring for the multitudes that come. History reveals that we will reproduce converts after our own kind. We will impart what we possess into those new believers.

I sometimes find myself praying, "God, don't fully release the harvest until You release something in Your church that is worthy of imparting to the multitudes of new converts. Don't allow another generation of easily offended Christians who lust for money, power, position, and pleasure to come forth. Please fill us with the knowledge of Your Son's splendor and loveliness before You bring hundreds of millions of new believers to us for training. Remember, Paul prophesied that the knowledge of Jesus would continue 'until' we *all* attain to unity, intimacy, and maturity" (Eph. 4:13).

THE PURPOSE OF THE ANOINTING

As my ministry was first being formed in the mid-1970s, I would look at some of the preachers and ask the Lord, "Why do You empower those evangelists who so overtly promote themselves?" The Lord assured me that the church in the End Times will have tenacious loyalty to the Person of Jesus.

> That I should preach among the Gentiles the unsearchable
> riches of Christ.
>
> —Ephesians 3:8, kjv

The Holy Spirit is looking for people who will preach the indescribable wealth of Jesus. He is not interested in establishing superstar personalities in the church. The Holy Spirit is looking to anoint men and women who will glorify Jesus in their personal lives when no one is looking.

God desires to release greater grace and power on His church. He will release this great power on those who proclaim the riches of Jesus' marvelous personality. (See Ephesians 3:8.) He will anoint believers who seek to capture the hearts of others for His Son—not for themselves.

Do you long to impact people for Jesus? Do you yearn to glorify Him in your personal life? Then I urge you to make the following two promises a top priority in your life. First, pray "that the Father of glory, may give to you a spirit of wisdom and of revelation in the knowledge of Him [Jesus]" (Eph. 1:17), and second, that the love wherewith the Father loves His Son would be imparted to your heart (John 17:26).

Read those two verses over and over. Meditate on them. Write down what comes to your mind as you pray them. Begin asking God for a spirit of revelation in the knowledge of Jesus' beauty. Ask that you might love the Son as the Father loves the Son. We must persevere in these prayers until we are "strengthened with power through His Spirit in the inner man" (Eph. 3:16). We will be restless until we become prisoners of God. As captives of His divine purpose, we will lead others unto passion for Jesus and into captivity to Him (Eph. 4:8).

I urge you to make being filled with the knowledge of the beauty of God's personality your life vision. Lose yourself in the pursuit of knowing Christ Jesus. Help others come to know in a deeper way.

As I said earlier, God is not interested in elevating super so they can build their own personal kingdoms. He is, however, committed to preparing a generation of righteous believers that are empowered by the indescribable loveliness of His Son. He will answer the heart cries of those who yearn to be filled with passion for Jesus. It takes God's power to break and melt hard hearts. Let's look at one way in which that will help.

CHAPTER 14

THE BLESSINGS OF INTIMACY

Some friends of mine remained childless after twenty-three years of marriage, much prayer, two major surgeries to correct infertility, endless rounds of testing and treatment, and the expenditure of thousands of dollars. Refusing to be spiritually barren as well, the couple had decided long ago to invest their lives in the kingdom of God by ministering to others. The wife earned a doctorate so she could serve God more effectively in her calling. The husband, a successful businessman, became salt and light through the political offices he held in the metroplex where they lived.

Then God surprised them. A courageous young woman canceled the abortion she had scheduled for the next day, carried her baby full term, and gave it up for adoption at birth, with the stipulation that the infant be placed in the home of a Christian couple who would rear the child for God. You guessed it. Through a series of divine coincidences and interventions, my friends, who hadn't even had their names on an adoption list because they were considered over the age limit to adopt, were blessed with a beautiful little boy just a few days old.

The elated couple understood that completing all the legal paperwork that established the baby's status as a member of their family was only a beginning. The greatest task lay ahead—that of establishing a deep, secure relationship of love between their adopted baby and themselves. They knew they would love their little son devotedly whether or not he ever returned their love, but they set out to win the child's love by demonstrating their love and affection for him.

Bathed in an atmosphere of love and stability, along with many hugs and kisses, their son became a picture of contentment and security.

Time passed, and one afternoon as the couple drove up in front of their home, their little boy exclaimed, *"My house!"* It was indeed. Everything that hard-working father and mother owned had been willed to him from the moment he had become a member of their family. All they had was his.

Then the day came when the couple's little son began to return their affection. His father kissed him on the cheek and whispered, "I love you," just as he had done a thousand times before. The little boy looked up, smiled, and said for the first time, "I love you, too!" The father's heart melted. He told this story to everyone whether they were interested in hearing it or not.

What he felt was just a small expression of what our heavenly Father feels when His children begin passing beyond the stage of self-centered receiving and start returning love back to Him.

We will never exhaust the fullness of the depth of love that God has demonstrated for us by making us His sons and daughters in His own house. As J. I. Packer writes in his book *Knowing God*, "The New Testament gives us two yardsticks for measuring God's love. The first is the cross (1 John 4:8–10); the second is the gift of sonship (1 John 3:1). Of all the gifts of grace, adoption is the highest."[1]

God the Father adopted you and me as His children, gave Himself to us as our loving Father, and made us fellow heirs with Jesus because He chose to, not because He had to.

THE MOTIVE FOR SPIRITUAL GROWTH

What best motivates a child to want to be like his parents? Is it affirmation and respect, or fear of rejection and guilt? Obviously, the children who are affirmed and feel secure will be the ones who most walk in the ways of their parents. The same principle is true in the spiritual realm. Using wrong motivations to encourage believers to pursue intimacy with Christ—fear, guilt, or manipulation—may seem to gain quick results, but those results do not last.

Even spiritual disciplines such as prayer, fasting, and Bible study, which are vital, can often result in legalism, pride, insecurity, or morbid introspection if pursued with the wrong motivation.

Christians will sometimes move into action faster if they are told God is angry and losing interest in them, or that they will miss out on the coming revival, losing everything that's dear to them on Earth if they do not get busy, performing and producing more for the kingdom. However, in the long run, some very sincere believers end up discouraged and burned out because they've built their spiritual lives on this faulty foundation.

The knowledge of God's deep affection and of our full acceptance as His beloved children is the best motivation for consistent spiritual growth. As Paul explained to the Roman believers, "You have not received a spirit of slavery leading to fear again, but you have received a spirit of adoption as sons by which we cry out, 'Abba! Father!'" (Rom. 8:15). Our spirits cry for more of Him when we begin to grasp the implications of being adopted as His children.

Being rooted and grounded in the Father's love is what best motivates us to greater consistency, spiritual passion, and maturity. As we begin to understand the Father's affection and the price Jesus paid to redeem us, our hearts melt with gratitude that leads us to devotion.

As you and I pursue intimacy with Jesus, it will become apparent that we are God's royal children. *We will manifest our family's likeness* by conforming to Christ. *We will seek to further our family's welfare* by loving our brethren. *We will maintain our family's honor* by avoiding what our Father hates, pursuing what He loves, and seeking His glory. As we cultivate intimacy with Jesus, out of the riches of His glory we will be "strengthened with power through His Spirit in the inner man" (Eph. 3:16).

SEVEN BLESSINGS OF HOLY PASSION

The first step toward experiencing intimacy with Jesus is our decision to pursue Him more than we pursue other good things, such as anointing in ministry, personal happiness, and success. When we set our hearts to seek the Lord, our lives will begin to change in many ways. Here are a few:

1. A focus on intimacy washes our hearts.

Jesus loved the church and gave Himself up for her "that He might sanctify her, having cleansed her by the washing of water with the word, that He might present to Himself the church" in glorious splendor (Eph. 5:26–27).

Just as you or I need a daily physical bath, we also need a daily spiritual bath to remove some of the "grime" and defilement. If the grime is allowed to accumulate, it will lead to spiritual dullness and insensitivity in our spirits. Inner corruption such as anger, slander, impatience, and sensuality grieves the Holy Spirit and makes our spirits insensitive and unable to respond fully to Him.

When we fix our hearts on the *Person* of Jesus and dialogue with Him, the Word of God washes our spirits. Defilement from our daily contact with a fallen world is cleansed away. The accumulation of information about the Scriptures and the mental discipline of hours of Bible study will never thoroughly cleanse the inner man in the way that devotional, worshipful meditation upon God's Word will. In Bible study alone, we store up important scriptural facts and concepts. But when our Bible study leads into personal dialogue with Jesus as we meditate upon His cleansing Word, we also experience growth in spiritual hunger, sensitivity, and nearness to Him. Active intimacy with His presence washes our spirits.

2. A focus on intimacy protects our souls.

We will never be empowered to walk in purity without the foundation of affection for Jesus. External disciplines and commitments to high standards of holiness without a living devotion for Jesus have little real power or life in them. A Person named Jesus—not rules and regulations—guards our souls. As affection for Jesus is increased in our hearts, we find a new empowering to resist temptation.

Let me share a practical example: When passion for Jesus is built into your spiritual foundation, it repels sensual communications that others may send your way. It returns the message, "No, I'm not available." That strong, clear message rises from within your spirit.

We are filled with such longing for Jesus that we have greater resolve to repel sensuality and resist wrong relationships. It is not a matter of being afraid that we might get caught. It is not an issue of fear that we might be shamed and lose honor, position, privileges, or even the anointing in our ministry. It is more than that. We have a higher motive for resisting temptation than a fear of AIDS or of coming under divine discipline. Our hearts are shielded by our love for Jesus.

The glory of the church is in our cleanliness, our purity. The soul aggressively engaged in pursuing intimacy with Jesus is positioned to overcome temptation. This is true even in natural relationships. It would be very strange for a person on her honeymoon to suddenly be swept off her feet romantically by a stranger. Most newlyweds are so preoccupied with the feelings they share with one another that the temptation to have an illicit affair on their honeymoon is absurd. On the other hand, the passive soul that wanders from fantasy to fantasy while living in a spiritual vacuum that lacks affection for God is much more vulnerable to fall to temptations that just happen to come along.

In our pursuit of intimacy with Jesus, we realize that feelings will come and go, sometimes swinging from the highs of holy passion to the lows of spiritual barrenness. We will have seasons of fervent longing and love for Jesus, times when we pray with great feeling and inspiration. But we will also experience seasons when we pray without any feeling of God's presence. Yet, as we persist, we will begin to realize that even in the dry, barren seasons our hearts are still growing in mature love toward Jesus. Our focus is on Jesus, not upon feelings that come and go.

As Paul declares, "The greatest of these is love" (1 Cor. 13:13). Love is our greatest motive. It is our greatest strength, joy, protection, and perseverance. The breastplate of Christ's love for us and our love for Him is the greatest piece of our spiritual armor. Only presumption dares enter into spiritual warfare without it.

3. A focus on intimacy motivates and inflames our hearts.

When we "sow to the Spirit" (Gal. 6:8), we expose ourselves to the presence of God whether we feel it or not. As focusing upon Him becomes the habit of our souls, we receive a greater release of life in our hearts

> For he who sows to his flesh will of the flesh reap corruption, but he who sows to the Spirit will of the Spirit reap…life.
>
> —GALATIANS 6:8, NKJV

The Lord invited the bride to position herself before Him that He might manifest Himself as a seal of fiery love on her heart. I have often asked the Lord to touch my heart with His presence as a seal of fire.

> Put me like a seal over your heart...
> For love is as strong as death...
> Its flashes are flashes of fire,
> The very flame of the LORD.
> —SONG OF SOLOMON 8:6

God's holy flame is relentless and consuming. It will eventually ignite one focused on Jesus with emotions of love for Him. However, if we are too busy to ask Him for this and to wait before Him for it, then this flame will be diminished. It's important that we understand this principle.

Also, we must understand that even though our careless living causes this flame of the Spirit to die down in our hearts, this does not mean God's love has decreased toward us. We must refuse to believe the subtle lie of the enemy that says God's love for us goes up and down with our own vacillating spiritual feelings and attainments. The flame we are referring to here does not represent God's love and affection for us; rather, it represents the passion and zeal that He imparts in us for His Son. We can lose our passion for Jesus without losing God's love for us.

4. A focus on intimacy satisfies our hearts.

Intimacy with Jesus is the context in which the deep longing in our hearts for more of Him is progressively satisfied. People who are born again do not automatically have a sense of the nearness of God. Effective ministry produces a satisfaction that comes through helping others and being useful in God's kingdom, but it is not the same as the satisfaction that comes from encountering God in our inner man. Nothing but an intimate relationship with Jesus will satisfy this inner cry birthed by the Holy Spirit.

The Holy Spirit may give spiritual gifts to believers and release His power through us, but these things do not ultimately satisfy the desire in our hearts for more of God. When our spiritual hunger is not being satisfied, we will experience frustrating spiritual boredom and restlessness.

5. A focus on intimacy frees us from insecurity and fear of man.

Intimacy with Jesus brings a deepened security and rest in our inner man. As we interact in a deeply personal way with Him, we grow in our knowledge that we are accepted and cherished by God. This knowledge progressively frees us from feelings of insecurity and the intimidating, paralyzing fear of others' opinions or actions against us.

A focus on Jesus ultimately leads us to an increased knowledge of His heart of affirmation for us. This is absolutely vital. As important as human affirmation is, it is woefully inadequate without a sense of God's affirmation of us. It is the knowledge that we are loved, accepted, and valued by God that gives us a greater sense of value and self-worth. When we are secure and confident in God's love, we grow out of our fears related to how people receive and treat us. When we know we are pleasing Him, the criticism that comes from others does not affect us nearly as much as it did in the past. "Proving" our value to others ceases to be the dominant drive in our emotional makeup. God's pleasure and His approving smile become the most powerful emotion that we have. This is a glorious way to live.

6. A focus on intimacy heals inner wounds of the heart.

God is raising up counseling ministries in the church today that provide a significant part of the process of our emotional healing.

Like almost everything that God restores to the church, counseling and inner healing have been abused and taken to extremes in many cases. But that does not mean these ministry tools should be shunned. The cure for abuse is *proper* use, not *disuse*. However, if we are to experience true, lasting wholeness and healing in the places of our wounding, we must encounter the Healer Himself and be encouraged to build a relationship of intimacy with Him.

Human hearts can be wounded in many ways. Almost daily we hear another tragic story of sexual, physical, verbal, or emotional abuse. Victims range in age from tiny infants to the elderly. Some of the stories of cruel inhumanity that I have heard seem to defy all limits.

When I think about this subject of healing of the heart, I cannot help but think of my brother, Pat. Few have been dealt a harder blow than he. After becoming a quadriplegic at the age of seventeen, he lost the most precious person in the world to him only eight months later when our father died, the first of many setbacks too many to describe here in detail. As I watched Pat fight an enemy that could be worse than paralysis or the death of a loved one, I saw him fight and win. Pat refused to allow bitterness to conquer him. It is supernatural how he has maintained his love for and trust in Jesus. He is unoffended at Jesus' leadership in his life. My brother is a champion of courage.

Now, thirty-three years later, he is still paralyzed from the neck down. But my brother's spirit is unhindered by the weights of self-pity and bitterness toward people or God. Over the years he has become a man of unusual humility and compassion, bearing the burdens of others. He counsels people by the hours, encouraging them to not give up on God. Watching his example has affirmed to me many times that an intimate relationship with Jesus can heal any wound in the human heart.

How are the inner wounds of the heart healed? That is an

extensive subject. Different ministries approach the answer to this in different ways. Regardless, all approaches must insist that God's people give everything back to Him, including all bitterness, self-pity, and desire for revenge. Our grief, anger, shame, and pride—even our hopes, dreams, and ambitions—must be laid on God's altar, along with our personal rights and the desire to run our own lives. Jesus must become the focus of our hearts—not our tragedies, our past, or all that might have been. Only Jesus can transform self-pity into victory or tears into triumph. A focus on intimacy with Jesus is essential in healing the inner wounds of the heart. My brother's life daily affirms this fact.

7. A focus on intimacy is an effective means of spiritual warfare.

Our greatest strength in spiritual warfare is also found in experiencing passion for Jesus. The enemy's strategy is to shift us from an offensive mode into a defensive mode where we're attempting to ward off temptation through sheer willpower and resolution. He fears offensive Christianity that pursues the Person of Christ and lives by the power of regular encounters with Jesus. I call this active intimacy with God. If Satan can separate us from our passion, then we become passive and aimless—easy prey for sin.

Let's look at two scriptural principles illustrating the wisdom of maintaining an offensive posture when dealing with the enemy: the principle of increasing and decreasing, and the principle of light and darkness.

THE PRINCIPLE OF INCREASING AND DECREASING

John the Baptist said about Jesus, "He must increase, but I must decrease" (John 3:30). This principle can be applied outside of its original context where John was allowing Jesus' ministry to replace his own. It also applies to how we grow spiritually as individuals. A proactive increase in our knowledge of God comes before we have the power to decrease in our bondage to darkness. That's God's divine order. Trying to decrease in sin when Jesus has not first increased within us is difficult and ineffective. Once the knowledge of God's personality begins to penetrate our hearts, it has a sanctifying, transforming impact on our emotions. As Jesus becomes more real to us, the inevitable result is a desire to give ourselves more to Him and to decrease those things in our lives that are working in opposition to Him.

THE PRINCIPLE OF LIGHT AND DARKNESS

We best combat spiritual darkness in our lives by receiving more spiritual light! John speaks of Jesus in terms of light: "In Him was life, and the life was the light of men" (John 1:4). John continues in verse 5, "And the light shines in the darkness, and the darkness did not comprehend it." John was declaring a very powerful spiritual principle: darkness cannot comprehend, and darkness cannot overpower light. Darkness is driven out of our heart by the entrance of the light of the revelation of Jesus. No darkness in the life of a sincere believer has the power to overpower the experience of God's light or revelation.

Attempting to drive the darkness out of our hearts by ourselves is frustrating and futile, but when the person of Jesus is unveiled to our hearts, that is when His light enters our hearts and the darkness flees. The same is true of natural light in a room.

How do we get rid of darkness in a room? It would be absurd to try to take buckets full of darkness out of a dark room. Rather, we simply turn the light switch on, and darkness is automatically overpowered. The presence of the light causes the darkness to flee out of the room. This principle applies to our spiritual lives as well. We will wear ourselves out by trying to remove darkness only by focusing on resisting it. Instead, we directly attack the darkness in our lives by focusing on receiving more light.

Satan is not intimidated by the boasts of believers who do not have an intimate relationship with Jesus. He knows that as long as darkness reigns unchallenged and unconquered in many areas of their own lives, those believers pose no real threat to his kingdom. Jesus is the One whom Satan fears. If believers are not filled with the reality and knowledge of Jesus, Satan knows it is only a matter of time until they will become victims of his attacks, not victors over darkness. Satan is troubled by believers who are undistracted from the purity and simplicity of devotion to Jesus.

> I am afraid, lest as the serpent deceived Eve by his craftiness, your minds should be led astray from the simplicity and purity of devotion to Christ.
>
> —2 CORINTHIANS 11:3

Satan flees before the sword of the Spirit when it is wielded by men and women who have a secret history in God of intimacy, faithfulness, and obedience. A focus on intimacy is an effective means of equipping us for spiritual warfare, for Satan is hindered by passion for Jesus, purity, and persevering prayer. The weakest, most immature believer who has a heart focus of holy passion will become a threat to Satan's kingdom.

INVITED TO INTIMACY

As we continue to focus on intimacy with Jesus, we will be rewarded and enriched by the release of these seven supernatural benefits in our lives. Let's review them once more.

1. Our spirits will be washed from defilement by the Word of God.

2. Our souls will be strengthened against temptation by the breastplate of faith and love affecting our emotions.

3. Our inner man will be motivated and inflamed by a release of divine hunger and zeal as our spirits are exposed to Jesus' flaming heart.

4. The deep cry in our spirits for intimacy with Jesus will be satisfied.

5. We will be freed from insecurity and the fear of man.

6. Inner wounds of the heart will be healed.

7. We will be equipped for spiritual warfare.

The choices are clear-cut: passion or passivity? Victor or victim? Blessings or barrenness?

We are invited to active intimacy with a real Person. For intimacy does not come accidentally. Intimacy comes through the hunger and yearning of our hearts and through sowing to the Spirit. As we hunger and thirst for Jesus, seeking Him and spending time in His presence, we grow more in love with Him.

CHAPTER 15

GAZING ON THE THRONE OF GOD

One of the reasons I love the Book of Revelation is that it keeps our time and purpose here on earth in clear perspective. It displays such striking contrasts: heaven and earth, time and eternity, evil and good, illusion and reality, lies and truth, the kingdom of light and the kingdom of darkness. Reading the Book of Revelation is a powerful reminder that this world is passing away. It sets our focus on the world that is to come. It reminds us of God's eternal throne. It reveals the majesty and eternity of Him who sits on that throne and the indescribable splendor of the glorious person who is seated at His right hand. Revelation 1:3 promises a blessing upon those who read the book, open their hearts to the things written in it, and seek to heed them:

> Blessed is he who reads and those who hear the words of this prophecy, and heed the things which are written in it; for the time is near.
>
> —REVELATION 1:3

During my early years of seeking to establish a consistent prayer life, I felt as though I were praying into the air—to some nebulous being far beyond my grasp. I had a feeling of disconnectedness, with no real sense of praying to a real person.

But over time, my prayer life has been greatly enriched through a simple devotional focus that I began some years ago. I call it "gazing on God's throne."

John describes the scene in heaven into which our prayers ascend. For example, he tells us what happens when we lift our voices and say, "Father, I love You." He paints a word picture of the setting to which our requests and petitions come. This description of God's throne, the Lord Jesus, the four living creatures, and twenty-four elders significantly changed my prayer life.

As Tozer said, "We must practice the art of long and loving meditation upon the majesty of God,"[1] that is, a reverent meditation on the Being of God. I took his counsel and began meditating upon the majesty of God. That's when the fourth chapter of Revelation opened up to me.

To aid my meditation, I studied Revelation 4 phrase by phrase, using the Bible itself as my commentary. Especially in the writings of Daniel and Ezekiel I found similar word pictures that made the scene John described even more vivid. (See Daniel 7:9–10, 13; Ezekiel 1; Matthew 19:28; 1 Kings 22:19; Revelation 5; 15:2; 20:4; Philippians 2:5–11.)

As I continued my study, the Person of God, heaven's throne room, and what happens there when we pray and worship and sing praises to God became more and more real to me.

I am not referring to using some counterfeit New Age visualization technique. Picturing the awesome scene John describes in Revelation 4 helps me enjoy holy fellowship with Jesus. Instead of "praying into the air," I often focus my thoughts upon the majestic Person seated upon His glorious throne, and I speak into His heart.

In Revelation 4:1 John says, "After these things I looked, and behold, a door standing open in heaven" (NKJV). In a vision the aged

apostle was able to gaze directly into the he
room. Read his awesome, eyewitness account:

> Immediately I was in the Spirit; and behold,
> heaven, and One sat on the throne. And He wh
> like a jasper and a sardius stone in appearance; a
> a rainbow around the throne, in appearance like   .
> Around the throne were twenty-four thrones, and on the thrones
> I saw twenty-four elders sitting, clothed in white robes; and they
> had crowns of gold on their heads. And from the throne pro-
> ceeded lightnings, thunderings, and voices. Seven lamps of fire
> were burning before the throne, which are the seven Spirits of
> God. Before the throne there was a sea of glass, like crystal. And
> in the midst of the throne, and around the throne, were four liv-
> ing creatures.... The four living creatures, each having six wings,
> were full of eyes around and within. And they do not rest day or
> night, saying: "Holy, holy, holy, Lord God Almighty, who was
> and is and is to come!"
>
> —REVELATION 4:2–6, 8, NKJV

Here is a picture of the throne of grace (Heb. 4:16). It is not a
throne of legalism or religion. God has invited all of His people to
come before this throne that they might receive mercy and find grace
to help them in their time of need. But it is much more than that.

This throne is an eternal reality. It will not become real when
we get to heaven and see it for the first time—it is real now. It does
not exist merely because we are in need, for it has existed from eternity past. It was secured in eternity before the heavens and earth
were ever created.

Jesus Christ's finished work on the cross has made it possible
for weak, broken people to come freely before this throne, with no
condemnation.

God the Father raised Christ from the dead, seated Him at His right hand in the heavenly places, put all things in subjection under His feet, and gave Him as head over all things to the church, which is His body (Eph. 1:20–23). The Lord Jesus is able to save forever those who draw near to God through Him, since He always lives to make intercession for them (Heb. 7:25).

The Spirit of God is constantly beckoning the saints on earth to live before the throne. One day we will joyfully cast our crowns before this throne. These crowns represent our spiritual achievements as we walked before the Lord in obedience and cooperated with the gracious work of the Holy Spirit in our lives (Rev. 4:10). But first we need to learn to cast our hearts before it in devotion and passion for the Son of God.

FINDING MEANING FOR OUR LIVES

This throne, filled with the grace of God, is the most awesome place in all existence. It is the foundation of the entire created order. It is the center of everything. It is the purpose for everything, for He who created all things sits upon the throne, and all things exist for His pleasure (Rev. 4:11).

When we stand before Him at the judgment seat, what He is thinking about us will be the only thing that counts. Once I understood that the only thing relevant to my life is what God thinks is relevant, then I had a clearer grasp of the meaning of my life.

Our lives only have meaning as we understand them with respect to obedience to Christ Jesus who is seated at the Father's right hand. If we lose our focus on Him, then we lose our connection with reality, purpose, and order. If we lose our vision of the throne of God as the center of everything we live for, then we lose our spiritual equilibrium and emotional stability. We lose our resolve to endure temptation and hardship (James 1:12). We lose our motivation to bless our enemies. We lose the main reason why God releases His power through our ministry.

When we lose the awareness of God our Father on this throne with Jesus seated at His right hand, then our problems become insurmountable in our thinking. The despair can seem unbearable. We forget that everything else passes away, and nothing has any significance and relevance outside the reality of the Person upon this throne. All else is temporal, except the things that are pleasing to Him.

THE FAMILY OF GOD

Notice how the angels and the twenty-four elders address God. They refer to Him as "Lord God Almighty, who was and is and is to come!" (Rev. 4:8, NKJV) and as "Him who sits on the throne" and "Him who lives forever and ever" (Rev. 5:13–14, NKJV).

But Jesus taught us to address Him as our "Father in heaven" (Matt. 6:9, NKJV). Paul reminded us that we have received a spirit of adoption as sons by which we cry out, "Abba, Father" (Rom. 8:15, NKJV).

The angelic host does not call Him "our Father." Only Jesus and born-again believers—the adopted sons and daughters of God who have entered into the blessed Father-child relationship with God on the grounds of Christ's work on the cross—have the privilege of calling Him "Abba, Father."

A WORSHIPING COMMUNITY

Jesus said to pray that His will would be done on earth as it is in heaven (Matt. 6:10). The community of God on earth—the church, the Father's family—is part of a larger community already in heaven.

Our family in heaven is filled with worship and adoration for God. They gaze upon the greatness, beauty, and splendor of Jesus on His throne. They deeply love the Son of God. The church on Earth is also to be a passionate, worshiping community existing to give ourselves wholly to Him. The purpose of both God's community in heaven and God's community on Earth begins and ends with worship around the throne.

It is tragic that so many Christians rarely come before this glorious throne. This does not mean that these believers are hypocrites. It does not mean that they are not interested in or indifferent to God. Many sincere believers long for a more satisfying relationship with God and are eager to experience His presence. However, they do not quickly connect this longing with God's requirement that we spend more time in His presence to receive more from Him. The lack of gazing on the throne that is so common in the church today means that so many are not being enriched by the grace of God in the way that God desires for them. Instead of living in contact with the awesome One seated upon the throne, many in the body of Christ are too busy, and thus they neglect this sacred privilege.

Many are unaware that God longs for us to receive a taste of the glory of His throne now—before we get to heaven. Consequently, today's church bears painful wounds that are the results of our negligence in this. The church cannot function properly when we neglect to encounter God's heart in this way.

When I am enjoying the Lord, I can feel mistreated by others without it bothering me nearly so much. But if I am not enjoying the intimacy of His presence, I am far more easily irritated and troubled. When that happens, I get off in a quiet place for a few hours and immerse myself in such classics as Tozer, Piper, the Puritan writings, or Psalms and the Song of Solomon. That practice is like a medicine, refreshing me and bringing my heart to peace and sometimes making it soar. Whatever was bothering me is not nearly as burdensome after touching God's presence.

At the International House of Prayer, we invite our interns to focus on intimacy with Jesus as an essential foundation in their spiritual lives. While one of the main functions of our prayer is to be intercessors, we also see to it that our weekly worship times are devoted to sitting at the feet of Jesus. This way we allow His Word to penetrate our hearts in a devotional way. We emphasize to our staff how important it is to spend time before the throne in adoration of Jesus as well as taking part in the intercession for revival and the breakthrough of justice.

Without the Person of the Lord Jesus as our central focus, without enjoying His presence regularly and thus having our hearts tenderized, we cannot function as a dynamic community with energy to serve one another and to fellowship in a deep way. Strife and division are the inevitable result when we attempt to draw real close to one another without also drawing close to Jesus. The only way the church can function according to design is for Jesus to be the active center of our life together. If we have lost that focus, then it must be restored.

In his vision, the apostle John describes four living creatures and twenty-four elders falling down before the Lord Jesus, the Lamb of God, "each having a harp, and golden bowls full of incense, which are the prayers of the saints" (Rev. 5:8, NKJV). I believe that the harps speak symbolically of our worship, and the fragrant incense refers to our prayers ascending before God's throne in the midst of myriads of angels.

John gives us a description of believers standing on the sea of glass worshiping in the midst of God's fire (Rev. 15:2).

Since we are seated in heavenly places with Christ (Eph. 2:6), learning to speak directly into the heart of a real, glorious Person seated on His throne in the heavens is one of the essential dynamics of inspiring devotional prayer.

I began to realize that, when we pray, we are not speaking nonchalantly into the air as if to no one. We speak into His very heart. We worship and speak directly into God's heart as we stand before His throne. Therefore, as I pray, I set my heart to talk to a real Person, offering my worship and prayers directly to Him. I picture myself standing on that sea of glass filled with fire as I gaze on the throne surrounded by the glorious emerald rainbow.

As I have continued with this focus, my prayer life has been enriched.

In the time that has transpired since I began this practice of gazing on God's throne, my problem of boring prayer did not suddenly forever disappear. However, it began to slowly change. I began to actually enjoy my prayer times. I even looked forward to them. I discovered that the hymn was right after all: "And the things of earth will grow strangely dim in the light of His glory and grace."[2] I never imagined that I would actually enjoy prayer. I know that if this happened in my spiritually barren prayer life, it will happen in yours as well. Just stay with it, and do not quickly give in and give up on this practice. I have seen many people at IHOP-KC begin to participate in regular prayer meetings. They confessed that they were beginning with a very dull prayer life; however, over time, yes, they did also change.

To encourage me in my journey to developing a sustained prayer life, I have made it a priority to read books or hear audio teachings that inspire me in prayer. For example, in my early twenties I heard a sermon that challenged me to read *The Life of David Brainerd* by Jonathan Edwards. Edwards was a well-known theologian living in the 1700s in America. Brainerd served as a missionary to the American Indians in the 1740s. The book turned out to be the single most influential book I've ever read outside the Bible.

Books on prayer written by people like E. M. Bounds and Leonard Ravenhill have greatly inspired me over the years. Also, books on the attributes and personality of God by people such as A. W. Tozer, John Piper, A. W. Pink, and J. I. Packer have been immensely helpful. I highly encourage you to read any of the works of Jonathan Edwards along with the devotional classics written by the Puritans.

HEAVEN'S THRONE ROOM

We are seated in heavenly places with Christ (Eph. 2:6). Do you ever imagine standing in heaven's throne room as you worship and intercede? Sometimes I whisper, "Oh, how I love You, Lord. Give me insight into Your glorious throne." Then, without saying a word, I simply gaze into the awesome scene that John the Apostle and other holy prophets of old have described for us.

I encourage you to pursue this astounding glimpse the Word of God gives us into this invisible world that rules our visible world. Picture a mighty throne, immersed in flames, standing in heaven. Imagine an indescribably glorious Person with hair and garments as white as snow, seated upon that throne. John described the Father's appearance as being like the brightness of a dazzling diamond (which was color of an ancient jasper stone) along with the fiery red color of the sardius stone. Picture a bright arch that looks like an emerald encircling the entire throne with a glorious radiance.

Think of the flashes of lightning and the peals of thunder coming from God's throne. Gaze in awe at the river of fire flowing from His throne. Daniel 7:9–10 describes a river of fire flowing from His throne, presumably into the sea of glass that is mingled with fire (Rev. 15:2). Picture twenty-four lesser thrones surrounding the great thrones on the right and the left and twenty-four elders clothed in white and wearing golden crowns sitting upon those thrones.

In front of the throne of Him who lives forever throughout eternity, imagine the flames of seven vast blazing torches—the sevenfold Spirit of God—reflected in an immense sea of transparent glass like crystal, mixed with fire.

The awesome, dazzling expanse of this clear, glassy sea mirrors the entire scene, creating a mirror image. Picture four living beings hovering around God's blazing throne. Listen as day and night these beings never cease to proclaim passionately, "Holy, holy, holy, Lord God Almighty, who was and is and is to come!" (Rev. 4:8, NKJV).

Do you hear the music or smell the fragrance? Let your soul think on the glorious music and the diverse fragrances that surround God's throne. Listen to the mighty roar of praise ascending from the myriads and myriads of angels on every side of the throne as together they cry out, extolling the Lamb who was sacrificed for us.

Look! Do you see Him? Jesus is there at the right hand of His Father. His loveliness and His splendor are beyond description. He is welcoming you to the throne of grace, smiling and bidding you to come. The mighty throngs of angels are parting to let you through, for they step aside softly when they see a child of God approaching.

Revelation 15:2 describes the place where we stand on the sea of glass mingled with fire. We stand here as we speak into His heart. That is the scene into which I come to offer my devotional prayers. And you can enter that scene in your prayer life also.

As we come there, day after day, year after year, our spiritual lives will be surely be enriched. Our spirits will be invigorated, and our minds will be renewed. We will be cleansed from the defilements of Earth as our souls are restored. The fruitless, temporal things of Earth begin to lose their hold upon us as we behold them from the perspective of that eternal, invisible world. And over the course of time we are changed—transformed—from glory to glory.

THE FIVEFOLD RESPONSE

John describes five specific actions being executed by the four living creatures and twenty-four elders in response to the Person seated on the throne:

> Whenever the living creatures give *glory* and *honor* and *thanks* to Him who sits on the throne, who lives forever and ever, the twenty-four elders fall down before Him who sits on the throne and *worship* Him who lives forever and ever, and *cast their crowns* before the throne, saying: "You are worthy, O Lord, to receive glory and honor and power; for You created all things, and by Your will they exist, and were created."
>
> —Revelation 4:9–11, nkjv, emphasis added

Notice the awesome activity taking place around the throne of God. The four living creatures are giving God glory, honor, and thanks. The twenty-four elders are giving Him worship and casting their crowns before Him.

I cannot claim to have captured a full understanding of the implication of any of these words and phrases. But I believe we need to take time to consider these five responses that flow out of the hearts of those nearest God's throne. Reflect upon the implications of these five responses for your life today.

1. Giving God glory

First, the four living creatures are continually giving glory to God. What does it mean to "give God glory"? How can you and I give Him glory? Paul said we "glory in Christ Jesus" (Phil. 3:3). In other words, we delight in the Person of Jesus. When we give God glory, we express our delight in and adoration of Him.

2. Giving God honor

What does it mean to give God honor? We honor Him through a life of radical obedience that backs up our desires to glorify Him. This means setting aside our own personal agendas so that we obey Him with our whole hearts. We demonstrate our respect and the value that we place upon Him by simply doing what He says. Jesus declared that we show our love for Him by obeying Him fully (John 14:21, 23).

3. Giving God thanks

Thanksgiving flows from a recognition that all our benefits come from *God's* goodness and commitment to *us*, not from *our* goodness or commitment to *Him*. We have not motivated God to love us; it is He who has motivated us to love Him. God gives us so much more than we give Him. When we grasp this, then our hearts are filled with gratitude. We recognize that God's goodness and generosity are the source of our blessings—not our dedication. Seeing who He is and what He endured and accomplished for us on the cross inspires our thanksgiving to Him.

4. Giving God worship

As we recognize His sovereignty, majesty, excellencies, and perfections, we will be utterly undone by who He is. As we see God's incomparable worth in relationship to everything else, our hearts will erupt and overflow in worship.

5. Casting our crowns before the Lord

The climactic response of the twenty-four elders' worship was to take off their golden crowns and cast them before God's throne. The crowns are an aspect of a believer's eternal reward as a result of his or her personal achievements through the grace of God.

When we stand before the judgment seat of Christ and our earthly lives are evaluated, all that was done for our recognition and all that was impure will be seen as wood, hay, and stubble, and thus will be burned up by God's fire (1 Cor. 3:11–15). Only that which was born out of our relationship with Jesus is of eternal value. It will be seen as gold, silver, and precious stones. This represents all that was Spirit-initiated and Spirit-sustained in our lives. It will endure God's fire as it passes through unscathed. Any treasures, any crowns we receive in heaven represent all we are and all we have attained as we cooperated with the work of the Holy Spirit in our lives. The crowns were forged in the costly, sometimes painful, fires of obedience, and they are ours forever. But we will have no desire to keep them for ourselves. Without hesitation, in extravagant abandonment, we will cast them at the Lord's feet.

Our spiritual attainments and rewards will not become idols in our heart because we will be in God's immediate presence. Paul reminded the Corinthians, "What do you have that you did not receive? But if you did receive it, why do you boast as if you had not received it?" (1 Cor. 4:7). Without God, we would be nothing and we could accomplish nothing.

When my two sons, Luke and Paul, were young, they inadvertently provided me with an "illustrated sermon" along this line. When Luke was about six and Paul was around four years of age, they came to me and said, "Dad, we don't have any money, and your birthday is coming up." So I thumbed through my wallet and handed them a five-dollar bill. (Then I thought it over and gave them another twenty dollars.) My sons took the money I gave them and went out to buy me a present. They came back and presented me with a brightly wrapped package, innocently assuming it was all a total surprise to me. Those two little guys were so excited. They could hardly wait for me to tear off the bow and paper and open the box.

As I pulled out the beautiful shirt they had chosen, exclaiming how much I liked it, I saw such pride and joy sparkling in their eyes. "We bought it for you, Dad!" they chorused. "Can you believe it?" Even though I had given them the money to buy the present, as I looked into their gleaming eyes, my heart, like theirs, was flooded with tremendous joy and satisfaction. I was overjoyed in their joy.

That's the way it will be when we stand before our heavenly Father. We will not think of it as "our" ministries or "our" successes and attainments that earned us glorious crowns. Those crowns will not have anything to do with the size of "our" ministry mailing lists or "our" prominence in ministry. Without our God, we could have done nothing. Yet our Father's heart, like ours, will swell with delight when we take off our crowns and present them to Him.

In the coming years, the Lord will give a great gift to the body of Christ. He will raise up an army of young leaders who know Him in a deep way. These young men and women filled with extravagant affection for Jesus will emerge to places of leadership in the church. Like Paul, they will "glory in the man Christ Jesus," not their ministries or how much impact or prominence they have gained. They will proclaim the Word of God and lead other believers into this same type of passionate affection for Jesus. Together on the last day, they will all cast their crowns before the One that they have dearly loved.

CHAPTER 16

Beholding the Glory Dimly

Back in my college days, I was trying hard to find the secret to a successful prayer life, but it was eluding me. I read a lot of books on prayer and the deeper life in God, but when it got down to actually praying, I was an absolute failure. I had carefully scheduled time to spend alone with God and was usually faithful to keep my appointments with Him. Yet my efforts at praying were frustrating, unfulfilling, and so boring. After months of drudgery and failure at praying and fasting, I told God, "Lord, I really love You, but I don't like praying. I hate fasting. And I don't like Bible study either because it is so boring. Other than that, I do really love You, Lord. But I do know that I'm not doing very well at walking with You."

I remember the condemnation and confusion I felt because I was striking out on the three "biggies" in my devotional disciplines. One thing that I did enjoy was attending worship services and hearing teaching. I loved to sing worship songs and hear sermons. I listened to thousands of Bible teachings on tape. I still remember the defeat I felt as I sighed, "Lord...will I *ever* like prayer? I do not know why talking to You is so boring."

I was living with three other Christian guys in a college apartment at the University of Missouri. We all worked together in a campus ministry. Each night around 8:45 my roommates would see me start getting uptight because I was dreading my hour of prayer from nine to ten o'clock. I hated going into my room to pray. I knew the next hour was going to be horrible, lifeless, and boring. But each evening at nine o'clock, there I'd be in dread. I would start the same way each time, praying something like this: "Lord, thank You for my arms and legs. Thank You for food to eat. Some people in poor countries don't really have much to eat—help them, Jesus. Thank You for my mom and for Pat. Thank You for my five wonderful sisters. Thank You for uhhhh...oh, yeah...thanks for letting me be on the college football team. Help me score touchdowns. Help us win. Uhhhh...oh, man, fifty-three more minutes to go! OK, let me see...hmmm...thank You for America. Help the president of the United States."

Sometimes I could hear a couple of my friends in the other room laughing at my dreadful routine. Every once in a while, they would poke their heads in and say, "Man, why don't you just relax?" I'd take a deep breath, square my shoulders as if I were about to tackle some giant, and mutter, "I'm gonna do this thing if it kills me!"

I was approaching prayer in all the wrong ways. I completely misunderstood the whole purpose of devotional prayer. Consequently, I dreaded prayer time. But I had made a vow to God that I would pray an hour every night, and I made up my mind to stick with it, regardless.

AS IN A MIRROR

One evening I was in my prayer closet, and, as usual, I'd completely run out of things to say in the first five minutes. I opened my Bible, searching for inspiration. As I read, it was as if a light dawned on my soul.

> But we all, with unveiled face beholding *as in a mirror* the glory of
> the Lord, are being transformed into the same image from glory
> to glory, just as from the Lord, the Spirit.
>
> —2 CORINTHIANS 3:18, EMPHASIS ADDED

My mind suddenly took off. Hmmm…as in a *mirror*…I am beholding the glory of God as in a mirror. What's a mirror? Well, a mirror gives a perfect reflection. Wait a minute. I learned that the mirror of the ancient world was very different from the mirror of the modern world. Today's mirrors give us a perfect reflection. But two thousand years ago when Paul was writing, the mirrors of that day did not even come close to giving a perfect reflection. Paul said, "For now we see in a mirror dimly…" (1 Cor. 13:12).

Dimly! An ancient mirror made of polished metal would give a faint, inadequate, very dim reflection. It was as if the Lord said, "Beholding Me dimly is all I have ever asked of you. If you do that, I will transform your heart."

The idea that even dim beholdings of God were sufficient to transform our hearts was a totally new idea to me. In other words, the dim beholding of uninspired prayer was sufficient to become transformed over time. I had assumed that all those boring, agonizing hours that I had spent in my little prayer room were all wasted and meaningless because I did not feel inspired or energized at all when I was praying. Somehow I had concluded that the only type of prayer that would transform me was prayer that I could feel God's presence. I thought that if I felt moved to tears by God's presence, then those prayers were dearer to God and thus more effective in changing me. I thought on my many hours of uninspired and unanointed prayers. I was imagining the Lord saying, "Yes, those prayer times were merely a dim beholding of My presence. But all that I have ever asked you to do in prayer was to behold Me dimly."

179

A dim beholding…as in a mirror, dimly… "Well, I can do that," I said to the Lord. "I can behold You dimly. Yes, sir, I'm an *expert* at beholding You dimly! That's been my problem." I was great at unanointed prayer times when I could not feel God. Yes, barely beholding God or dimly discerning His presence was the way I usually prayed.

The truth was dawning on me. Even seemingly unanointed, uninspired praying is significant to God! "This is fantastic!" I shouted. "I can do this! It's a progressive process. If I continue to pray—even those dim, difficult prayer times will change me. I'm slowly being transformed from glory to glory!"

I ran out of the prayer room and made the announcement to my startled roommates. "Guess what, you guys? Unanointed prayer is relevant!"

"What?"

"Unanointed prayer is relevant! It works! It doesn't matter if it's anointed. It doesn't matter if it's inspired. An uninspired, dim devotional life is relevant to God!"

That became my main message everywhere I went. Some of my friends on campus just shrugged and said, "Bickle is off on some weird kick about unanointed prayer!"

I don't think they ever really understood what I was trying to say. Maybe I did not explain it very well. But that was all right. My heart had grasped God's liberating word of hope to me. I knew if I persevered in prayer—even dim prayer—there was absolutely no doubt about it: I would gradually be transformed!

BEHOLDING GOD'S BEAUTY IN HIS EMOTIONS

So what is the glory of God that we are invited to behold, however dimly and with our imperfect understanding and partial revelation? God's wisdom and power are evident to anyone with even casual familiarity of the Bible, and both are amazing expressions of His glory, but I firmly believe that God's emotions reveal to us the clearest picture of what His glory looks like. When the Spirit transforms us from glory to glory as we behold the glory of God, we are beholding the emotions of this beautiful God.

Moses was one of the great students of God's emotions. He prayed to see God's glory (Exod. 33:18) and secured two promises from God: that God's goodness would pass before him, and that God would proclaim His name to Moses. What is God's name but His personality and what He is like? The Lord made this clear enough when Moses asked His name in Exodus 3:13. The I AM is not only how He feels, but also what He thinks and what He is.

When God reveals Himself and fulfills these promises a few short verses later, He passes by Moses and tells him, "I am the Lord, the Lord God. I am merciful. I am gracious. I am longsuffering. I am abounding in goodness." This was God's answer to Moses' plea to see His glory. He told him what He was.

The Lord's mercy that He ascribes to Himself when speaking with Moses is evident in His dealings with David. Not only was David fast to repent and eager to be reconciled with God, but he instantly ran back to the safety of God's mercy. Unlike many people, David did not sit in a puddle of self-pity and resist God's mercy. In the ugly aftermath of sin, he relied fully upon God's tender mercy and loving-kindness, secure that God would blot out his transgressions (Ps. 51:1). This was the glory of God, there to behold. His glory is His mercy, and His mercy is a part of who He is, a part of His character and personality.

Jesus displays the goodness that God attributes to Himself, quoting His Father's discourse with Moses and saying, "Father, I will proclaim Your name to them." (See John 17:26.) He goes on to reveal why He will proclaim His Father's name to the disciples: so that the love with which the Father loves the Son would be imparted to them. A study of God's personality and emotions will awaken supernatural love for God within us.

Looking on God's emotions and His beauty was David's life goal (Ps. 27:4), and it is a noble example to follow. Beholding is becoming, and as we look upon the Lord, we will begin to reflect His very character and disposition. We love God because we understand, or because we behold, that God first loved us (1 John 4:19). The love that He feels for us inspires reciprocity in our own hearts.

This principle works in all aspects of God's emotions. Whatever we behold in God's heart is awakened in our own, and we are able to give it back to Him. How do you become passionate for Jesus? You become passionate for Jesus by becoming an avid student of Jesus' passion for you. How do you enjoy God? Seek to understand the way in which God enjoys you. You will pursue God when you realize the unyielding way in which He has pursued you. The same goes for yearning, for delight, for joy, for any of God's emotions. When we understand in our minds what God is truly like—the glad Father who delights over us and the relentless judge who will not suffer the presence of filth in His beloved—then we gain a true picture of God and His emotions. He will work in our hearts to transform us into a reciprocal lover.

AN UNVEILED FACE

I want to focus on two key elements in the phrase "But we all, with unveiled face beholding as in a mirror" (2 Cor. 3:18). The first element in coming to God with an unveiled face refers to coming with a confidence rooted in understanding the finished work of the cross. In Old Testament times, veiling the face was a way of signifying the great gulf between a person and God and the need for a mediator. God through Christ has invited us to come fearlessly to

His throne of grace (Heb. 4:16). We come without a sense of condemnation or accusation because Christ took our penalty and gave
us the gift of righteousness.

A second element to this phrase "with unveiled face" refers to
honesty of heart. No deception. No false façades or religious jar-
gon. No cover-ups or excuses. We can open our hearts to the Lord
and speak plainly of our failures, hurts, disappointments, fears,
and frustrations. Thus, we behold the glory of Jesus with *unveiled
faces.*

FROM GLORY TO GLORY

Most of us do not discern the glory of God that is actually present
with us. Often I have overlooked the work that God was doing in
and through me. I identify with Zerubbabel. His story of overcoming discouragement is hinted at in the Book of Zechariah.

After seventy years of captivity in Babylon, the Jews were
allowed to return to Israel. Zerubbabel was appointed as governor of the new group of exiles that we see returning to the
land. Zechariah, a young prophet of priestly lineage, stood at
Zerubbabel's side to provide prophetic encouragement to him.
When the people reached Jerusalem, they first set up the altar of
sacrifice to the Lord. Then they proceeded to lay the foundation
of the new temple amid the massive ruins in the city of Jerusalem.
Let's read Zechariah's account:

> So he answered and said to me: "This is the word of the Lord to
> Zerubbabel: 'Not by might nor by power, but by My Spirit,' says
> the Lord of hosts. 'Who are you, O great mountain? Before
> Zerubbabel you shall become a plain! And he shall bring forth
> the capstone with shouts of "Grace, grace to it!"'" Moreover the
> word of the Lord came to me, saying: "The hands of Zerubba-
> bel have laid the foundation of this temple; his hands shall also

finish it. Then you will know that the LORD of hosts has sent Me to you. For who has despised the day of small things?"

—ZECHARIAH 4:6–10, NKJV

From here, let me give you the Mike Bickle paraphrase of Zechariah 4:6–10:

Zerubbabel had tried to get people to work on rebuilding the temple, but they were so discouraged that no one would work. So the disheartened governor sat down on a huge stone, looking around at the heaps of rubble from what had once been a great temple before the Babylonian army destroyed it in 586 BC.

"Jerusalem is in total ruins," Zerubbabel sighed. "There is nothing left of this city. Toppled stones and debris everywhere. This place is a disaster."

Just then, young Zechariah, the prophet, tapped Zerubbabel on the shoulder. He said, "How's it going in your work to rebuild the city and temple?"

"What a disaster!" moaned Zerubbabel. "Nobody showed up for work again today. Here I am, 'the great restorer of the land of Israel.' We are supposed to raise up this temple to the glory of God, but I cannot get any one inspired to work on it."

"Zerubbabel, God is with you."

Looking up at the young prophet, Zerubbabel questioned, "God is with us?"

"Of course He is. The very fact that you are in this city and no longer in captivity is proof of that. God says that your hands have laid the foundation of this house, and your hands will finish it. But there's something you have to do first."

Zerubbabel moaned and shook his head.

"No, no. Listen to me. See that stone over there almost hidden by grass and weeds? That's the capstone, the finishing stone for the new temple. It's the final stone the people will put into place, the stone that signifies the building is completed."

"Yeah, OK. So?"

"Well, God says you're to shout, 'Grace, grace!' to it."

"To what?"

"To the stone."

"I'm supposed to shout at a stone?"

"Listen to me, Zerubbabel. God said to tell you, 'It is not by might, nor by power, but by My Spirit.' You're supposed to put your confidence in the grace of God. That's what shouting 'Grace!' is all about. Come on now. Get up, walk over there, and shout, 'Grace! Grace!'"

"Zechariah, I know you mean well. But I'm already having trouble getting people to follow me. If they see me standing out here in the middle of these weeds, shouting at a rock—"

"Zerubbabel, are you going to obey the Lord or not? Are you going to trust His grace, or aren't you? Now say it!"

"OK. What have I got to lose? I'll do it. Here goes: 'Grace... grace...'"

"No, no, that will never do. Shout it, man! Like this: Grace! GRACE!"

After a couple of halfhearted shouts, both stood silently looking at the stone. Finally Zechariah said, "You know what's the matter with you, Zerubbabel? You despise these days of small beginnings."

Zerubbabel made no reply, and Zechariah continued, "Because you do not see a lot happening around you right now, you're counting these days as unimportant. You have thrown them away as irrelevant. But the very fact that you're here in the land is the beginning of the move of God. There is something very great He wants to perform."

"It doesn't feel like the move of God to me."

"That's because you're out of touch with how God sees it. You are despising what is happening now because it looks small. It is small, but it is also real; it is legitimate. All these obstacles that look like great mountains will become a flattened plain. You'll see the day when this temple is complete and the capstone is set in place. Why wait until that great day when the last finishing touch is put on the temple before you begin to see the validity of your work? Begin praising God right now, and trust Him that your efforts are relevant even in this day of small beginnings."

What happened to Zerubbabel when he was rebuilding the temple happens to many believers in the building of their own spiritual lives. They make the mistake of thinking that they are wasting their time because they do not see or feel that much is being accomplished when they begin seeking God and meditating on His Word.

But being transformed from glory to glory is an operation of the Holy Spirit on the inside—in our minds, wills, and emotions. It is being strengthened with power through His Spirit in the inner man (Eph. 3:16).

There's a false notion among many Christians that the Word of God works only if you have ten hours a day to be shut up in a room all alone reading it. But the Word of God was written primarily to the 99 percent of the human race who will never be in "full-time," salaried positions of ministry.

God's promises are not just for paid preachers. They are also for the everyday person on the street, the stressed-out mother dealing with a toddler stuck in the terrible twos, the truck driver, the clerk at Wal-Mart, the secretary, the businessman, the schoolteacher, and the courtroom lawyer. God's Word is for the believer who fell into sin and lost everything except a heart that still cries out for God.

Every Christian—any Christian—can be progressively transformed from glory to glory. The problem is our idea of glory. We have this idea that it's not glorious unless we experience the full blinding glory of God radiating from His throne in heaven. Some people cannot discern the reality of the presence of God's glory. The glory of God is not limited to a burning-bush encounter with God. It's not, as some people mistakenly think, either the full glory or no glory at all. Being transformed from glory to glory is a promise made to every believer.

We can experience an ever-increasing measure of that glory in the small, subtle dimensions that often go unnoticed.

Suppose you are a new Christian. The fact that you think differently now than the way you did before you were saved is the beginning of the glory of God at work in your life. Before your conversion you may have rarely thought about what pleased God. Now you have a deep interest in the things that delight Him. That is the beginning of the glory of God in your life. It's not a small thing. It may be only a beginning, but it counts to God!

Some believers have progressed to the next stage of spiritual maturity. They hunger to grow in their prayer lives. They long to be able to understand the Scriptures. They try to minister the life of Jesus to their families or to people at work. Although they fail, the sheer presence of those desires is a valid manifestation of God's glory in their lives. It is proof of the work of the Holy Spirit in them. Do not despise the small beginnings of the Spirit's work in your heart.

The very fact that we are pained by condemnation reveals a deeper longing in us to do what pleases God. Before we were saved, we did not struggle with condemnation because we were not trying to please God anyway. We must not minimize the value of our holy desires to obey God. Yes, we failed in our obedience, but the very fact that we are seeking to obey is a vast difference from how we

lived while unbelievers. Our desires for obedience are a manifestation of the ever-increasing glory of God working in our lives.

The point I'm making is this: Some people's definition of the
glory of God is so out of reach that they think they will never
experience it. Consequently, these believers come to the conclusion
that God is not real or that salvation does not really work. Yet all
the time it was working in them in a small way, but they did not
have the discernment to comprehend it. Like with Zerubbabel,
the rubble of the past is being cleared away. Slowly but surely, a
foundation in God is being laid in our lives. Someday a beautiful
temple will rise from the ruins of our broken lives. Begin shouting
"Grace! Grace!" right now. Do not wait until the job is complete.
Have confidence that even now "He who began a good work in you
will perfect it" (Phil. 1:6).

Never underestimate the grace of God or despise the day of
small beginnings. We should not say, "I'll never be different. I will
always be in bondage to lust, anger, and covetousness. I'll never be
free." The glory of God is already at work in your life. Thank Him
for the sincere desire you have to break free from sinful habits and
walk in the Spirit. Those small beginnings are firm steps in the
direction of full maturity.

CHANGED AND STILL CHANGING

Change is a difficult process. If we are faithful in taking little steps,
we will gradually experience transformation. We will be transformed into Christ's image in an ever-increasing splendor and from
one degree of glory to another. Dim beholding is a fruitful beholding. It's a small beginning, but it is a true beginning.

Throughout church history God's people have tried to reduce
the process of transformation to a mechanical set of spiritual aero-

bics. Roman Catholics and some evangelical denominations alike have their own versions of this sanctification machinery.

Here's the good news. Sanctification and transformation come from beholding—not from *striving!* I jumped through every religious hoop I could find, but it was not until I began to *behold* a Person that my heart was transformed.

Paul was zealous for spiritual things beyond all his contemporaries (Gal. 1:14; Phil. 3:4–8). But when he beheld the glory of Jesus, he was transformed. Martin Luther exhausted himself trying to perform religious exercises that were prescribed for his holiness. But one day he had a revelation of God's grace, and both he and the church have never been the same since.

Part of the Christian world has dived headlong into a never-ending cycle of recovery, self-help, and how-to-do-it sermons, books, and tapes. Some of the material is helpful, but most neglect the one important principle: transformation does not come from striving or from psychological techniques alone. Transformation comes from beholding the glory and splendor of Jesus, who is a real Person.

Many people make solemn spiritual resolutions about what they will begin to do from now on or about what they will never do again. But unless God touches our hearts with His presence, we will never change. We may drag ourselves into the prayer room on a regular basis, but only God can change the heart. It happens by His grace working in us. We must put ourselves in a position to receive the grace of God. We must put our frozen hearts before the bonfire of His presence until our hearts warm up and thaw out. Paul referred to God's grace as the source of all his accomplishments:

> But by the grace of God I am what I am, and His grace toward me did not prove vain; but I labored even more than all of them, yet not I, but the grace of God with me.
>
> —1 Corinthians 15:10

Over three decades have passed since that night in my college apartment when "the light came on" for me—that dim beholding in regard to praying without needing to feel inspiration. Over the years, I've stuck with my schedule, adding more time with the Lord as my hunger for intimacy with Him has increased. For me, regular prayer time, Bible reading, and fasting are not exercises to earn God's favor. The merit badge mentality is gone, and my relationship with God is no longer performance-oriented. The transforming power of my devotional life is in the beholding, even though I only behold Him dimly. I actually enjoy prayer now, and it's good. I can even handle the unanointed times. I love reading, meditating, and studying the Word. Therefore, witnessing to unbelievers about the grace of God is a joy. I have even come to appreciate how fasting can sharpen my focus on the Lord and eternal things.

At International House of Prayer of Kansas City we have discovered that prayer joined together with worship results in making prayer enjoyable. Thus, it is much easier to engage in prayer for long periods of time. In addition to that, praying together in the company of hundreds of other like-minded intercessors also makes the goal of a living a life sustained by prayer more attainable. When surrounded by encouragement and people who are experiencing exactly what you are going through, the unanointed times of dryness seem easier to get through.

So many things have changed for the good inside me. I now enjoy the spiritual disciplines I used to despise. Over the years I have discovered a stronger resistance in my heart toward some of the sinful things I once loved. I still find some things in my emotions and thinking that I do not like. I believe the Holy Spirit will strengthen and transform my inner man in those areas as well.

It is as if I gain victory over certain sinful areas that are evident when the Spirit's "microscope" is set to a magnification power of ten. But when the power of the Spirit's magnification is adjusted to one hundred, then I see new depths of my carnality. The closer I get to the Lord, who is light, the more darkness I am able to see in my heart. I am not discouraged by that, because the darkness was always there; I just did not see it as clearly years ago. As I continue in my fellowship with Jesus, beholding Him through the Word and in prayer, the process of transformation will continue. I am confident that Christ will continually be more fully formed in me (Gal. 4:19).

So remember: Despise not the day of small beginnings. Honor God for every transforming step, no matter how small or insignificant it seems to the natural mind. Do not let uninspired prayer get you down or make you stop seeking the Lord. A "dim beholding" is all God has required of us. Dim beholdings are fruitful beholdings. Those dim beholdings, in time, will be sufficient to transform us from glory to glory!

CHAPTER 17

WASTING YOUR LIFE ON JESUS

To the southwest of Jerusalem lies a deep, narrow ravine with steep, rocky sides, known as the Valley of Hinnom, or "Gehenna." On the southern brow overlooking the valley, King Solomon built an altar to the god Molech, who was honored through the fiendish custom of sacrificing infants to the fire gods. In this valley Ahaz and Manasseh, kings of Judah, sacrificed their sons as sacrifices, burnt offerings, making them "pass through fire." The horrible practice seems to have been kept up for a considerable period of time.

King Josiah attempted to put an end to these abominations by polluting the idol altars, rendering them ceremonially unclean. From that time, Gehenna appears to have become the common cesspool of Jerusalem. The city emptied its sewage into the valley to be carried off by the waters of the brook Kidron. Fires were kept burning in the valley to consume the solid waste deposited there. The valley was filled with an overpowering stench and served as a receptacle of waste, refuse, and all that defiled the holy city. It became symbolic of the place of waste, destruction, and everlasting punishment. Jewish apocalyptic writers began to call the valley the entrance to hell. Later, its name Gehenna became synonymous with hell itself.

The word *Gehenna,* occurring twelve times in the New Testament, is always translated as "hell." It is the name for the eternal abode and place of final punishment for Satan, his evil forces, and the wicked. Jesus Himself often used the term in reference to the destiny of the lost and as an awesome warning of the consequences of sin.

In view of those facts, I think of Jesus' words in John 3:16. Most of us can quote that familiar verse by heart: "For God so loved the world, that He gave His only begotten Son, that whoever believes in Him should not perish, but have eternal life." When we say "should not perish," we automatically think of eternal destruction in hell. Yes, it is true that Jesus proclaimed a message that could deliver mankind from perishing in that fiery trash heap called "hell," where all that would defile God's holy city—the New Jerusalem—are cast.

But when Jesus said "should not perish," He also meant that He wants to keep us from another kind of perishing—from wasting and throwing our lives away now, here on Earth.

Many believers are leading futile, meaningless, frustrating lives. Oh, they're going to heaven, all right. But in the meantime, they're literally wasting God's gift, throwing away the precious hour God has granted them on Earth.

God created mankind with tremendous capacities and abilities. Speaking of man, it says in Hebrews: "Thou hast crowned him with glory and honor, and hast appointed him over the works of Thy hands; Thou hast put all things in subjection under his feet" (Heb. 2:7–8). God intends marvelous things for the redeemed. He desires that we be transformed into the image of His Son and that we make an impact for Him on the lives of others during our brief stay on Earth.

Your life won't be wasted in eternity. But that doesn't stop Satan from trying to get you to waste the life you're living now on Earth. He wants you to fail and fall short of your potential in God. Jesus never intended believers to perish in any dimension of the word—in this life or in the one to come. If Jesus said whoever *believes* in Him should not perish, why then do we see so many Christians perishing in this life by squandering their earthly time and talents?

We must understand that the word *believe* means much more than a one-time reach to God in a desperate moment. The word *believe* implies a continual process of reaching out to God in faith and obedience, not only to avoid eternal destruction in hell, but also to avoid wasting our lives on Earth by experiencing God's purpose now.

I want to do the extravagant thing for God. Out of love and gratitude I want to go beyond that which is required. I want Him to reap His full inheritance that is intended from my life. How tragic, how grievous, how unnecessary it is to waste our life in this age through carelessness, passivity, and desire for other things.

We must be watchful. We must stay spiritually wide-awake. We must not lose our focus or become trapped in wrong relationships. The kingdom of God is worthy of our watchfulness. We must not cultivate any desires that would hinder or quench our spiritual lives, lest on the day of judgment we suffer loss and our lives be judged unfruitful and wasted (1 Cor. 3:15).

MISUNDERSTOOD EXTRAVAGANCE

It's a strange thing, but when we seek with all our hearts to fully do God's will, our families, friends, and even leaders in places of spiritual authority (the very people who should know better) often misjudge and criticize us.

For example, the religious leaders of Jesus' day ridiculed and opposed Him, and His own brothers and sisters misjudged Him (John 7:5). If those things happened to Jesus, why should those who seek to fully obey Him expect anything different?

We expect the world's value system to be way off-center, putting power, money, and prestige above everything else. But the value system of the church is off-center as well. For example, many Christians consider it unfortunate when a young believer with a bright mind or financial success chooses to bypass certain privileges and promotions in order to live his or her time and life in God more fully.

Many Christians disdain those who choose to live simply, pouring their resources into the kingdom of God instead of spending it on lavish lifestyles for themselves. Some believers criticize and look down on Christian mothers who choose to stay at home and invest their lives in their children instead of in careers, clubs, and clothes. Examples of the worldly value system that has invaded the church are all around us.

I remember the negative things that were spoken to me when, after being accepted to medical school, I turned it down to go into the ministry. Some of my friends thought I was being foolish and fanatical. They knew that being a medical doctor had been my goal for years. "Mike! You—a pastor? What a waste!"

God did not first call us to be "successful" in the earthly sense, but our first call is to be *faithful*. God does not measure success by sacrifice, salary, or university degrees; He measures it by obedience and faithfulness. The world, and even some in the church, may look at you, shake their heads, and sigh, "What a waste!" But in the end you will enjoy God's smile and His reward.

WHY THIS WASTE?

A woman whom I consider to have been one of the greatest saints in the New Testament was condemned for being "wasteful." The devotion she displayed for Jesus has strengthened my own resolve many times. I love her faith, courage, and sensitivity to the things of God. I look forward to meeting Mary of Bethany in the eternal city some day.

The facts we have regarding Mary are few. She was the sister of Lazarus and Martha. She lived in Bethany about a mile east of the Mount of Olives in her sister Martha's house. She and her sister first appear in the tenth chapter of Luke, where Jesus commends Mary, who sat listening eagerly for every word that fell from His lips. She had "chosen the good part," "the one thing needful," while "Martha, cumbered about with much serving," was distracted by all her preparations. (See Luke 10:38–42.)

The next mention of Mary is at the death and resurrection of her brother, Lazarus. After that we see Mary once more in Scripture. About a year had passed since the time Jesus had been a guest in Martha's home and she had complained, "Lord, do You not care that my sister has left me to do all the serving alone? Then tell her to help me" (Luke 10:40). Now, just days before His crucifixion, Jesus had returned to Bethany.

On this occasion, Jesus was a guest in the house of Simon the leper. Matthew tells us that Mary, Martha, and Lazarus were present. John adds, "They made Him a supper there, and Martha was serving" (John 12:1–2). I believe that in Martha and Mary we have represented the two types of people in the body of Christ. Both are valid. Both are diligent. Both are loved by Jesus Christ. And both can get out of balance. One is the service-oriented believer, and the other is the communion-oriented believer. The body of Christ would not function well without either one.

John 12:1–9 and Mark 14:3–9 describe what took place in Bethany at the home of Simon the leper. Jesus, Lazarus, and the others were reclining at the table, and Martha was serving. That very day Jesus had told His disciples that after two days, the Passover would be coming, and He would be delivered up for crucifixion (Matt. 26:2), yet His words seem to have fallen on deaf ears. Everyone was sitting around eating, drinking, and chatting merrily. Hadn't anyone heard what Jesus had said? Hadn't anyone understood?

From what happened next, it appears that one had. Without warning, Mary appeared, clutching an alabaster vial containing a costly perfume—a pound of pure nard worth three hundred denarii, a year's wages. Before anyone could stop her, Mary, following a Jewish custom where wealthy people anointed the bodies of their loved ones with costly oil before burial, broke the vial and began pouring its precious contents over Christ's head and anointing His feet. The next moment she was on her knees before Him, wiping His feet with her hair as the perfume's fragrance filled the entire house.

For an instant everyone in the room sat dumbstruck. Then their stunned silence was shattered by the angry objections of Judas Iscariot: "Why was this perfume not sold for three hundred denarii," he demanded, "and given to poor people?" (John 12:5). John reveals the protesting disciple's true motives and intentions: "Now he said this, not because he was concerned about the poor, but because he was a thief, and as he had the money box, he used to pilfer what was put into it" (v. 6).

Judas was not the only person criticizing Mary's extravagant display of devotion. Others present were also scolding her. Mark says they were "indignantly remarking to one another, 'Why has this perfume been wasted?'" (Mark 14:4–5).

That is often the reaction of people who "like" Jesus but do not deeply love Him. Anything above the minimum, anything of special value offered to Him—whether it be a remarkable musical talent, a brilliant mind, or one's whole heart—is regarded as unnecessary wastefulness. Mary's devotion stands in sharp contrast to the shallow commitment of such followers of Christ.

When you begin to love Jesus as Mary of Bethany loved Him, sooner or later you will receive scolding from others. Mark my words. Just because people have big names, big positions, and big ministries does not always mean they have hearts full of affection.

Around that table in Simon's home, all the clamor quieted as Jesus began to speak. Surely He would reprimand Mary for her recklessness. After all, hadn't the Teacher taught about the prodigal son who wasted his substance with riotous living and about the steward who wasted his master's possessions? After feeding both the four thousand and the five thousand, hadn't Jesus instructed His disciples to gather up into large baskets all the leftover fragments of bread and fish that nothing might be wasted? Surely Mary was about to receive the sternest reprimand of her life!

Jesus' response stunned the group almost as much as Mary's actions had:

> But Jesus said, "Let her alone; why do you bother her? She has done a good deed to Me. For the poor you always have with you, and whenever you wish, you can do them good; but you do not always have Me. She has done what she could; she has anointed My body beforehand for the burial. And truly I say to you, wherever the gospel is preached in the whole world, that also which this woman has done shall be spoken of in memory of her."
>
> —MARK 14:6–9

"Let her alone, Thomas. Stop scolding her, Matthew. Philip, don't say another word to her. Judas, Peter, sit down. Mary's true heart has been revealed, just as your own are soon to be. I know exactly why she did what she did, and it was a good thing. This woman has done all she could do for Me."

Today, many Christians do not even recognize all the names of Christ's twelve apostles who were present and probably scolding her on that occasion. But we are still hearing sermons about Mary of

Bethany and her act of devotion, just as Jesus said: "Wherever the gospel is preached in the whole world, that also which this woman has done shall be spoken of in memory of her" (Mark 14:9).

Both Mary and Martha ministered to Jesus that day. Going to great lengths to prepare a banquet worthy of the Master, Martha served her Lord a natural feast. Mary prepared Jesus a spiritual feast, something He could enjoy and feast on just two days before He endured the worst hours in His entire existence—from eternity past to eternity future. Mary gave Jesus something from her heart that He could carry with Him to the cross.

GIVING WITHOUT REGARD TO COST

There are no Bible verses that say we all must empty our bank accounts, close the doors of our businesses, and give it all to the poor. Never make the mistake of thinking Jesus demands extravagance in our love to Him. He requires only the simple giving of our hearts in faith and obedience, the taking up of our own crosses and following Him.

Some wealthy people can enjoy the luxury of giving money or making a purchase without regard to cost. They may never have to look at a price tag. They can waste the money if they want to because they have so much.

They will not feel the financial effects of spending too much on a car or a dinner. It makes no difference, because they still have plenty left over. But this was not the case with Mary. For the rest of her life, Mary would feel the financial effects of her costly sacrifice in this act of devotion to Jesus. Yet this woman broke her most precious earthly treasure and joyfully lavished it upon Him. Why? Because Jesus was the most priceless treasure to Mary. She understood that His body was about to be broken for her.

How do you suppose a young woman like Mary had acquired a bottle of perfume worth a year's wages? Nothing in these passages indicates that Martha, Mary, or Lazarus was wealthy. But the fact that the house mentioned in Luke 10 is referred to as Martha's house does imply several things. Either Martha was a widow and had inherited the house from her deceased husband, or the parents of Martha, Lazarus, and Mary may have died, leaving the house to Martha since she was the eldest. (If Lazarus had been the eldest, by Jewish custom, the house would have gone to him.) It also makes us wonder if the costly perfume might have been left to Mary as part of the inheritance from their deceased parents. If so, the perfume probably represented Mary's financial security for her future. We have no way of knowing these things for sure, but some things are certain: the perfume belonged to Mary, and it was very expensive.

I'm sure that concerned friends and relatives later approached Mary asking, "What about tomorrow, Mary? You have no security now."

I can imagine her replying, "I have Him, and that's good enough for me. My future is in His hands. Over a year ago Jesus told me I had chosen the good part, which would not be taken away from me, and I'm putting my trust in what He said." (See Luke 10:42.)

FRIENDSHIP WITH JESUS

On each of the three occasions where Mary appears in the New Testament, she is pictured as sitting at the feet of Jesus. (See Luke 10:39; John 11:2; 12:3.) Based on the depth of devotion for Jesus we see in Mary's life, is it any wonder that Jesus loved Mary, Martha, and Lazarus and cherished their special affection and friendship?

Bethany was only a mile or so from Jerusalem, a twenty-minute walk. Six days before the Passover, Jesus made that walk to Bethany, to the home of Mary, Martha, and Lazarus.

Why did He choose to spend the last six days of His life on Earth with them? Why not with Nicodemus, a leading Pharisee, "a ruler of the Jews" and a member of the Sanhedrin, the spiritual and political senate of Israel? Jesus could have used that time to pour His strategies and purposes into this influential man, building him up spiritually, enabling him to stand firm in his strategic position during the trying days ahead.

Why did Jesus not stay with Silas or with Barnabas, leaders in the early church from its beginning, men who lived in Jerusalem and who would later travel and minister with the apostle Paul? Why did He not stay in the home of Joseph of Arimathea, a wealthy disciple who could have financed many things for the Jerusalem church, or with Matthias, who would later be chosen to occupy the ministry and apostleship vacated by Judas Iscariot? Why didn't Jesus go to the place where His own mother was staying?

Out of 120 intercessors in the upper room on the day of Pentecost, why did Jesus choose to spend the remaining days of His life in the home of Martha, Mary, and Lazarus? I believe His main reason was that these three friends loved Him with great devotion and firmly believed in Him. Their house was a sanctuary of peace, affection, and rest. It was a place where He could relax, feel loved, and be strengthened for the grievous days ahead.

Martha and Lazarus were Jesus' good friends. Mary was a person who felt what Jesus' heart was feeling. Her attentive ears were able to catch the meaning of His veiled words. She was a friend who never partook in the disciples' arguments as to which of them was the greatest, who never requested the privilege of sitting at His right hand in the kingdom. She was simply Mary, His devoted friend. She realized what an inestimable privilege it was just to sit at His feet, bask in the beauty of His presence, and drink in His every word.

Mary may have never been anointed to preach or to perform signs and wonders, but she was anointed with a tender heart of love. The Scriptures never record that Mary of Bethany had a prominent ministry like some of the others. But during Christ's final days before Calvary, this woman's worshipful spirit must have ministered greatly to the Son of God.

WASTING OUR LIVES ON JESUS

None of us have an option when it comes to whether or not our lives will be wasted. The only option we have is *how* we will waste them. All of us will waste our lives either in sin and compromise, passivity, and the cares of this life, or we will waste them on Jesus. We can waste our lives on serving the devil and end up in a flaming trash heap called hell. Or we can waste our lives and our resources on Jesus as Mary did, laying up treasure in heaven where moths and rust won't corrupt it and thieves cannot break through and steal it. O God, give us grace to live as Mary did.

Jesus loves the world and the church, but there is a special grace that He gives to those who seek to love Him in an extravagant way, to those who waste their lives on Him. How do you waste your life on Jesus? It's no secret. Get a vision to live this way. Then spend time in His presence. Reject sin. Cry out to Him in prayer. Fill your heart with the Word until it is filled with the things that fill God's heart. Abandon yourself to Him. Intimacy with God takes time, and there is no substitute for waiting in His presence. Like Mary, choose to forgo some of the less important things going on around you to make more time to cultivate a relationship with Him. Rearrange your schedule to make time for Him.

Why don't you take my hand and come with me just for a moment? Stand here and gaze through the door John opened for us into that invisible world. It is the world you and I will be living in tomorrow—the world where we will be living ten billion years from now.

There! Do you see it? A rainbow-encircled throne! Seated upon the throne is the One who lives forever and ever. Amid the seven lamps of fire burning before the throne do you see those living creatures? Can you hear them crying, "Holy, holy, holy"? Watch now! When the living creatures give glory, honor, and thanks to Him who was and who is and who is to come, the twenty-four white-robed elders will prostrate themselves before the throne, worshiping God.

Do you see Him? The Lamb who purchased men for God with His own blood and made them to be a kingdom and priests to God. He is there. Look! Listen! Surrounding the throne, the living creatures, the elders, and the Lamb are thousands and thousands of angels, and they are all crying, "To Him who sits on the throne, and to the Lamb, be blessing and honor and glory and dominion forever and ever" (Rev. 5:13). Do you hear them? Can you see that great cloud of witnesses, composed of believers of all the ages, assembling as one mighty nation?

Would you like to walk up before the throne and bow down? We can. We do not have to draw back in fear or shame. There beside the Father is Christ, our high priest. He understands our weaknesses and infirmities. He sympathizes with our liability to the assaults of temptation, for He has been tempted in every respect as we are, but without sinning.

There's no need to be timid. We're not trespassing on forbidden ground. We have actually been *invited* to come here. I've read the invitation myself, and it says we may *fearlessly, confidently, boldly draw near* to God's throne of grace that we may receive mercy for our failures and find grace to help us in our time of need (Heb. 4:14–16).

Since we have been invited, I come to the throne often to meditate, to gaze, to expose my spirit to the majesty and eternity and holiness of our glorious King and to put earthly things into eternal perspective. I bring my needs and cares, my confessions and commitments, my appeals and my attainments and present them to Him. I watch as they rise like sweet-smelling incense before the Lord. May the Lord fill you with passion for Jesus.

NOTES

CHAPTER 3

IS YOUR GOD TOO SMALL?

1. J. I. Packer, *Knowing God* (Downers Grove, IL: InterVarsity Press, 1973), 6.

2. A. W. Tozer, *The Knowledge of the Holy* (New York: HarperCollins Publishers, 1961), 76.

3. Ibid., 23.

4. Ibid., 129, 131.

CHAPTER 4

BECOMING FASCINATED WITH GOD'S BEAUTY

1. Wikipedia.org, "Martyr," http://en.wikipedia.org/wiki/martyr (accessed December 19, 2006).

CHAPTER 5

FROM INTIMATE KNOWLEDGE TO PASSIONATE LOVE

1. William Wordsworth, "The World Is Too Much With Us," in *Sound and Sense*, Laurence Perrine and Thomas R. Arp (Orlando, FL: Harcourt Brace Jovanovich College Publishers, 1992), 46–47.

CHAPTER 7

"KISS THE SON LEST HE BE ANGRY"

1. C. H. Spurgeon, *The Treasure of David: An Expository and Devotional Commentary on the Psalms*, vol. 1 (Grand Rapids, MI: Baker Book House, 1983), 11.

CHAPTER 8

STRONGHOLDS OF THE MIND

1. Tozer, *The Knowledge of the Holy*, 6.

2. Ibid.

CHAPTER 14

THE BLESSINGS OF INTIMACY

1. Packer, *Knowing God*, 194.

CHAPTER 15

GAZING ON THE THRONE OF GOD

1. Tozer, *The Knowledge of the Holy*, 123.
2. "Turn Your Eyes Upon Jesus" by Helen H. Lemmel. Public domain.

WHAT IS THE IHOP-KC MISSIONS BASE?

It is an international missions organization committed to **prayer** (intercession, worship, healing, prophesying, etc.), **fasting** (covering 365 days a year), and the **Great Commission** (proclaiming Jesus to all nations with power as the way to establish His **justice** in the earth). Our work includes equipping and sending missionaries as dedicated intercessors and anointed messengers working to see revival in the church and a great harvest among the lost.

IHOP-KC MISSIONS VISION STATEMENT

To call forth, train, and mobilize **worshiping intercessors** who operate in the forerunner spirit as End-Time prophetic messengers. To establish a 24-hour-a-day prayer room in Kansas City as a perpetual solemn assembly that "**keeps the sanctuary**" by gathering corporately to fast and pray in the spirit of the Tabernacle of David as God's **primary method** of establishing justice (full revival unto the great harvest). To send out teams to plant Houses of Prayer in the nations **after** God grants a breakthrough of His power in Kansas City. The forerunner spirit operates in God's grace in context to the fasted lifestyle (Matt. 6) and prepares others to live in wholehearted love by proclaiming the beauty of Jesus as Bridegroom, King, and Judge.

VISITING IHOP ON WEEKENDS

Encounter God Services: Weekends at IHOP-KC—renewal, conviction, refreshing, impartation, and equipping are what we pray to be released in these weekend meetings at IHOP-KC. On **Friday nights**, Mike Bickle teaches on themes related to intimacy with God. On **Saturday nights**, he teaches on themes related to the End-Times. On Sundays, join the IHOP-KC staff for worship and teaching. Childcare is available. **One-day seminars** are taught on Saturdays.

*See **www.IHOP.org** for details, visitor's accommodations, and more information on joining our staff or attending our internships or Bible school.*

Visit IHOP-KC at www.IHOP.org

The International House of Prayer Missions Base Web site has been designed for ease of browsing. We have incorporated the following branches of our community into one cohesive site:

- *IHOP*
- *Onething*
- *Children's Equipping Center*
- *Forerunner School of Ministry*
- *Forerunner Music Academy*
- *Joseph Company*
- *Events & Conferences*
- *Internships & Training Programs*
- *Omega Course*

It's all located at our easy-to-remember address: *www.IHOP.org*. Whether you are interested in visiting IHOP, receiving the Missions Base podcast, browsing the bookstore, watching live Webcasts, or enrolling in FSM's online eSchool, the Web site delivers the information you need and offers many opportunities to feed your heart. With login capabilities that expose you to even more comprehensive IHOP materials, we hope our site will become an ongoing resource for many years to come. Some of the Web site features include:

- *Podcasting*
- *MP3 Downloads*
- *Forums*
- *Free & Subscription-based Webcasts*
- *Sermon & Teaching Notes*
- *eSchool Distance Learning*
- *Internship Applications*
- *Prayer Room Blogs*
- *Online Bookstore*
- *And More!*

Visit us soon at www.IHOP.org!

IHOP INTERNSHIP PROGRAMS

IHOP offers a variety of three-month and six-month internships for all ages. Each internship has the same basic components, including prayer meeting attendance, classroom instruction, practical ministry experience, community fellowship and team building, conference participation, practical service, and Bible study. Internship attendees regularly participate in prayer meetings—between fifteen and twenty-five hours a week—in the prayer room, which can include worship team involvement, intercession for revival, personal devotional time, and study of the Word. Education and instruction cover a wide range of topics, including Christian foundations, prayer, worship, intimacy with God, the Bridal Paradigm of the Kingdom of God, the prophetic and healing ministries, serving the poor, and many others.

Intro to IHOP is a three-month internship for people of all ages, married or single, who want to learn and experience all that IHOP represents—prayer, worship, intimacy, etc.

Simeon Company is a three-month training program for people ages fifty and older who refuse to retire in their desire to radically serve Jesus through prayer, fasting, and worship.

Onething Internship is a six-month daytime internship for young adults between the ages of eighteen and twenty-five who are singers, musicians, intercessors, or evangelists. This program includes housing and eighteen meals a week.

Fire in the Night is a three-month nighttime internship for those between the ages of eighteen and thirty who want to worship and minister to the Lord through the night, midnight to 6:00 a.m. This program includes housing and eighteen meals a week.

Summer Teen Internship is a three-week summer program to equip teens in prophetic worship, intercession, and intimacy with Jesus. Housing is provided with IHOP-KC families.

Please visit *www.IHOP.org* for more information.

FORERUNNER SCHOOL OF MINISTRY

*Redefining Theological Education
Through Night and Day Prayer*

FOUR PROGRAMS:
- Apostolic Preaching Program
  Four-Year Program
- Worship and Prayer Program
  Four-Year Program
- Healing and Prophecy Program
  Two-Year Program
- Biblical Studies Program
  Four-Year Program

ONE ACADEMY:
- Forerunner Music Academy (see below)
  Three-Year Program

THREE INSTITUTES:
- Joseph Company
- Apostolic Missions Institute
- Evangelist Institute

CTEE:
- eSchool – offering access to
  Video/Audio/Class Notes

FORERUNNER MUSIC ACADEMY (FMA)

FMA is a full-time music school that trains musicians and singers to play skillfully and to operate in the prophetic anointing. FMA offers a comprehensive course of high-quality musical training in the context of IHOP's night-and-day prayer and worship. King David understood that prophetic music and songs would release the power of God. He paid 4,000 full-time musicians and hundreds of prophetic singers to gaze night and day upon God as they sang the prayers of Zion. This was their primary occupation in life. They were employed in the Tabernacle of David, which combined worship with intercession that never ceased as it continued 24/7.

CONTACT US:
12444 Grandview Road
Grandview, Missouri 64030
Phone: 816.763.0243
Fax: 816.763.0439
E-mail: FSM@ihop.org
www.IHOP.org

OTHER RESOURCES BY MIKE BICKLE

AFTER GOD'S OWN HEART

This book gives in-depth insight with many practical examples of how to sustain a life of intimacy with God. King David's relationship with God is used as a model of how we can live a radical lifestyle filled with confidence before God while acknowledging our profound weakness.

THE SEVEN LONGINGS OF THE HUMAN HEART

God has placed deep longings in the heart of every human being. We all long for beauty, for greatness, for fascination, for intimacy. We all long to be enjoyed, to be whole-hearted, to make a lasting impact. Only God can fulfill the longings He has given us. When we realize our longings are godly and God wants to fulfill them, we find freedom and joy.

THE REWARDS OF FASTING

Fasting is a gift from God that goes way beyond not eating. Jesus promised we would be rewarded for fasting. Done in the right spirit, fasting increases our receptivity to God's voice and His Word and allows us to encounter God more deeply than we otherwise would. This book explores all the rewards and delights that come to those who fast.

THE PLEASURES OF LOVING GOD

This book invites you on a most unique treasure hunt, a journey of discovery into intimacy with a Bridegroom God that loves, even likes, you and wants your friendship. Dimensions of the forerunner ministry and the House of Prayer are also examined.

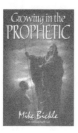

GROWING IN THE PROPHETIC

As churches across the country struggle to determine the proper place for the prophetic in their congregations as well as guidelines for the operation of prophecy, the lessons learned by Mike Bickle provide a starting point.

ENCOUNTERING JESUS AUDIO SERIES

"A Prophetic History & Perspectives About the End Times." Over the last twenty years, Mike Bickle has taken time to share bits and pieces of this prophetic history but never as comprehensively as he did in these twelve one-hour sessions! These experiences explain the prophetic history of this ministry in Kansas City as well as establish convictions about the generation that the Lord returns. Although Scripture is our highest standard and guardian of truth, on occasion, the Lord also releases prophetic experiences to encourage our understanding and perseverance.

SONG OF SOLOMON AUDIO SERIES

Mike's completely revised and updated course on Song of Songs, this is his most comprehensive and powerful presentation on this glorious book to date. The CD version includes the Study Guide in PDF format.

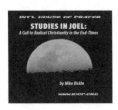

STUDIES IN JOEL AUDIO SERIES

As we approach the great and terrible day of the Lord, we will be facing a flood of horrors far greater than in the days of Noah. In his brilliant verse-by-verse teachings from the book of Joel, Mike blows the trumpet and sounds the alarm, offering us a road map of the End-Times.

RESOURCES FROM FORERUNNER MUSIC

ALWAYS ON HIS MIND — Misty Edwards

"Diving deep into intercession, into the Word, into the passionate heart of God." From IHOP-KC, *Always on His Mind* is a live recording that captures Misty Edwards and her team leading worship, intercession, and songs born out of prayer.

CONSTANT — IHOP-KC

Constant is an album that is steady and lyrically inspiring! This collection of songs is thematic of the faithfulness of God. His greatness and our great need for Him are sustained throughout. All the music on this album was written and performed by the International House of Prayer worship leaders.

MERCHANT BAND — Merchant Band

With sounds of Brit pop meets American rock, Merchant Band's self-titled debut album has woven a modern sound with the IHOP messages of intimacy and urgency. Packed with original material that is both fresh and powerful.

ETERNITY — Misty Edwards

This best-selling CD captures the heart of the extravagant worshiper. Misty Edwards is one of the International House of Prayer's most beloved worship leaders. Her unique gifting draws your heart before the Lord, our Majesty, into a deep realm of intimacy with Him.

LIMITED EDITION — IHOP-KC

Connect to the Prayer Room Through Limited Edition

Through IHOP's *Limited Edition* CD subscription club, Forerunner Music now offers you an ongoing glimpse into the International House of Prayer's prayer meetings. We record the worship and intercession that goes on night and day at IHOP. Then we take the best recordings from a two-month period, compile them, and make them available to you. Join IHOP's worship leaders and prayer leaders as they keep the prayer fire burning 24/7.

As the name suggests, these CDs are "limited editions," meaning once we've sold out, no more are available. And the CDs are only available to subscribers. Join the *Limited Edition* CD club, and every other month you will receive the latest CD, as well as other news from the prayer room and regular email updates.

Each *Limited Edition* CD is packed with live worship and prayer. You will find your heart connecting to Scripture and with IHOP's current prayer burdens. We invite you to join us as we seek after the fullness of God. Enter into fiery, passionate intercession with recordings from our corporate intercession sets or sit at the Lord's feet through a Worship With the Word or Devotional set recording. Our desire is that the *Limited Edition* CDs will equip and bless you as you draw nearer to the One you love.

For more information about resources from Mike Bickle and the International House of Prayer or for a free catalog, please call 1-800-552-2449 from 8:30 am–5:30 pm Monday–Friday. Also, visit our Web site and Web store at www.IHOP.org.

Learn More About
God's
Incredible Passion for
You!

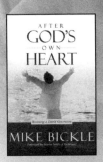
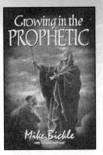
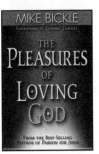